That's It, I Quit

That's It, I Quit

◆

A Guide to Quitting Smoking Forever

Dean F. Giannone, M.D.

iUniverse, Inc.
New York Lincoln Shanghai

That's It, I Quit
A Guide to Quitting Smoking Forever

iUniverse, Inc.

For information address:
iUniverse, Inc.
2021 Pine Lake Road, Suite 100
Lincoln, NE 68512
www.iuniverse.com

ISBN: 0-595-29046-9

Printed in the United States of America

Contents

Introduction

So, you finally decided to quit smoking cigarettes. Excellent decision. As I'm sure you know, smoking is a very bad habit, fraught with negative health and societal consequences. One of the best things a smoker can do to improve his or her overall health is to quit smoking. Many professional medical organizations, as well as quite a few of your friends and relatives, I'm sure, have strongly recommended you stop smoking. Quitting smoking is a great thing to do.

Just don't expect it to be an easy thing to do. If you haven't already attempted smoking cessation, be prepared for a difficult challenge. If you have already tried and failed, you've experienced the difficulties first-hand. Very few people who have quit smoking will tell you that quitting was easy. Even if they do, talk to them again in a few months and see how they're doing; chances are they'll be smoking once again.

The fact is, quitting smoking cigarettes is a grueling challenge, rife with both short- and long-term struggles. You may never end fighting the urge to buy a new pack of cigarettes and start your smoking life anew. Your life may be studded with several failed attempts at cessation.

Now, don't think you're alone in your decision to quit smoking. And certainly don't think you're the only smoker to find quitting difficult. Of the 47 million smokers in the United States, about 32 million want to stop smoking. If it were easy to stop, there would only be 15 million smokers in the United States, right?

But don't worry, it's not completely hopeless. You're not relegated to a life of cigarette smoking. You are capable of quitting, of living a life without cigarettes, of putting your bad habit behind you forever. You may just need a little help along the way, that's all. Like any great challenge in life, you need some instruction before you attempt to conquer it. You would never think of jumping out of an airplane with a parachute without some formal instruction by an experienced jumper. You would never attempt to ride a bucking bronco without some training by an experienced rodeo professional. And it's certainly not acceptable to have to face the daunting task of smoking cessation alone.

In this book, I provide you with education and understanding about the habit of smoking. Through my years of medical practice, I've come to appreciate the simple fact that people can overcome adversities much more easily if they under-stand the reasons behind the adversities. People are much more likely to achieve success after discussion than after instruction. For example, if a patient goes to a doctor with a sinus infection, he would be given an antibiotic. The doctor would prescribe the antibiotic, and instruct the patient to take the antibiotic for four-teen days. Now say that patient starts to feel better after the fifth or sixth day. Not knowing otherwise, this patient may stop taking the antibiotic and put it in the medicine cabinet for the next time he or she comes down with an infection. A few weeks later, the infection will likely return because of an incomplete cure.

On the other hand, if our patient goes to a doctor with a sinus infection, the doctor prescribes an antibiotic for fourteen days, and the doctor explains that the infection may recur, and become even more difficult to treat, if the patient stops the antibiotic prematurely, the patient is much more likely to complete the four-teen day course of antibiotics. In this context, the patient understands the impor-tance of a fourteen day course of antibiotic despite feeling better after the fifth or sixth day. The patient will complete the full fourteen day course of therapy, and the infection will be cured. With discussion comes understanding. With under-standing comes success.

The reason understanding and discussion breed success is because, as someone who has accepted a challenge, you will know what to expect along the way. Try finding your way around an unfamiliar town without a road map. Try assembling an entertainment center without an instruction sheet. You have decided to quit smoking, which is wonderful, but you may not know what obstacles are present along the way. If you know of the obstacles ahead of time, you can prepare your-self to conquer them. Preparedness breeds success. Understanding breeds success. Discussion breeds success.

This book, then, is a discussion of the challenges you can expect to face in your quest to stop smoking. Among other things, we will discuss:

- Why cigarette smoking is so bad for you.

- Why even second-hand smoke is terrible for your health.

- Why even your own brain wants you to keep smoking.

- What are the ingredients of a cigarette, some of which you would never con-sider ingesting alone.

- What are the best techniques for quitting, and which ones don't work at all.

- What alternative therapies work, and which ones don't.

- What to do if you read this whole book, do everything I say, and still fail.

By understanding the concepts discussed in this book, you will be prepared to face the obstacles between you and your goal of smoking cessation. You will understand why you smoke, why you shouldn't smoke, and how to stop effectively. This will give you the best opportunity for success. Discussion, understanding, preparedness, success.

Now I know you're probably wondering if I ever smoked in my life. No, I haven't. But as a physician, I've seen the worst of illnesses caused by smoking. I've seen too many people die because of smoking-related illnesses. I want to contribute to stopping the epidemic of smoking. I want to contribute to stopping the deaths. Please read this book carefully and completely; it has all the tools and knowledge you need to quit smoking forever.

Why People Smoke

Why do you smoke? Simple question, right? Not really. You see, your reasons for smoking now are likely quite different from those that started you smoking in the first place. So in actuality, this question actually has two parts: why did you start smoking, and why are you smoking now? But then again, you can't conceptualize yourself at only two points in time, can you? You've grown over the years, and changed continuously over that time. You've evolved into the person you are today. So we also need to consider how you evolved as a smoker in order to understand why you smoke today. So you see, the question as to why you smoke is rather complicated.

In order to understand why you smoke now, we need to delve a bit into your personal history to investigate why you started smoking in the first place. There is usually a great difference between the reasons for starting smoking and those for continuing to smoke. Certain circumstances, or pressures, triggered your smoking behavior some time ago. By addressing these original issues regarding smoking, you'll discover that, for the most part, they don't apply anymore. The circumstances surrounding your initiation of smoking behavior have likely resolved long ago. If those issues have dissipated, the question remains, then, as to why you still smoke.

In this chapter, we will work through a series of questions regarding your past and current use for cigarettes. These questions will force you to think about the reasons behind your desire to smoke. They'll seem like simple questions, but in fact, you may have some trouble answering them for me. By working through them thoughtfully and honestly, these questions will hopefully help you to understand what, if anything, cigarettes currently mean to you. In other words, we will attempt to define a significant role that cigarettes play in your life currently. If none is found, then you have all the more reason to quit.

Why did you start smoking?

Do you remember your very first cigarette? Did you take a cigarette from someone, or did you buy a whole pack yourself? What was happening at the time that made you smoke that first cigarette? Were you with anyone, or were you alone? What truly drove you to smoke that very first cigarette? There are several reasons implicated in the initiation of smoking behavior, all emerging from the fields of sociology and psychology. Don't get me wrong, I'm not saying that smokers are nuts. The initiation of smoking behavior usually occurs at a young age, is dependent on social and family interactions, and is ingrained in the creation of an individual's identity. People typically start smoking in their teenage years, or sometimes at an even younger age. Some reviews have documented significant numbers of children as young as eleven years old smoking on a regular basis. But what forces drive such youngsters to start smoking. Certainly not the same forces that drive an adult to continue to smoke. Do such youngsters suffer from job stress? They shouldn't even have jobs that cause them stress. Would these youngsters prefer to enjoy a cigarette with their favorite drinks while in the company of friends? Well, cigarettes are not usually grouped with milk and orange juice, and I would hope children of this age aren't drinking beers with their friends. So what issues drive youngsters to smoke? The answer lies in the creation of one's identity.

As youngsters, we all strive to create an individual identity for ourselves. We may want to be noticed, or we may wish to fade into the woodwork. We may try to be popular with certain groups, or we may care to be left alone. We wear our baseball caps backwards, rip holes in our jeans, buy concert T-shirts, or shave our heads. We join the swim team, learn to play a musical instrument, attend wood shop, or take up a foreign language. We do these things to define ourselves in society, to find a niche in which we belong. And one of the things that some of us do in this search for an identity is start smoking.

But, how do we begin to construct an identity for ourselves? How to we decide how we wish to be perceived by society? Well, the decisions surrounding the creation of one's identity are borne through experience with society-attending school, going to the movies, spending time with family or friends, and watching television, to name a few examples. The things we see, and feel, and learn during these interactions help us to manufacture ourselves, so to speak, into the people we long to be. We place these experiences on a metaphorical assembly line in which we're lying on a conveyor belt, rolling along, slowly being built into what we imagine as our ideal selves. I'll provide a few examples to illustrate how the initiation of smoking behavior integrates into this assembly process.

Let's talk, first, about you best friend from elementary school. He's the coolest! In fact, you're going right now to meet him at the video arcade. You jump off your bicycle, lock it to the bike rack, and open the door to the arcade. You look around, and finally spot your best friend playing Pac-Man in the corner. You can barely make him out; he's surrounded by other kids who are watching him play. But he's fairly tall, and his unmistakable New York Mets baseball cap, which he always wears backwards, pokes out above the throng. You run over to him, standing on your tiptoes to catch a glimpse of him playing. It looks like he's going to get another high score today. He's a master at Pac-Man; he always beats you when you play against him, but you love hanging out with him so you just accept defeat and enjoy the experience. He always draws a crowd when he plays; he's very popular, and you like to share in his popularity.

He finally finishes his game-yet another high score. Everyone in the gathered crowd pats his back and slaps his hand. He emerges from the crowd and, seeing you, runs over to give you a big noogie. He emotes about his new high score. You tell him you have a surprise for him and, unbuttoning your jacket, reveal your new Led Zeppelin T-shirt. Your friend can't believe it; he loves Led Zeppelin. Inside, you already know he loves Led Zeppelin; that's why you bought the shirt in the first place. The fact is, you hate Led Zeppelin. He then tells you he has a surprise for you. He leads you out the back door to an alley behind the arcade. There, you see a small crowd of kids from your class standing in a circle under a strange white cloud. As the two of you walk over, your friend shouts out to the crowd. The circle opens to engulf the two of you. Once in the circle, you see that all of them are smoking cigarettes. Curious, you turn to your friend just in time to see him flick a lighter and light a cigarette of his own. He jokes and laughs with the other kids, while you stand baffled, not realizing that your friend smokes cigarettes. You've never smoked a cigarette before. What do you do now?

In this first example, you find the image that your friend has created appealing, and you wish to emulate that image. You desire the same positive response from your peers that he's able to provoke through his choice of clothes, activities, and music. That's why you insist on wasting quarters playing Pac-Man even though you always lose. That's why you purchased a Led Zeppelin T-shirt when your favorite rock group is Air Supply. And that's why you'll probably turn your baseball cap backwards and walk into the nearest deli to buy your first pack of cigarettes.

As a second example, let's talk about your big sister. You love your big sister. She's so much fun! On this day, she bounds home from school with a few of her friends, books in hand, and boys following. The crew marches through the living room to the kitchen, in which your parents eagerly await. Today is report card day, and they have expected your sister's arrival. Smiling ear to ear, your sister produces her report card to your parents. An A+ average, once again. The Dean's List, once again. One step closer to the college of her choice, just in case being one of the best lacrosse players in the state doesn't earn her a scholarship. Your parents beam; they hug your sister for an eternity. She turns to high-five her friends, then bends down to give you a big hug, never neglecting to include her little sister in any festivities. She's the best!

Your parents announce that they'll be treating the whole bunch to pizza. As they call the pizzeria, your sister and her friends run up the stairs to her bedroom. As you listen, eight pairs of feet ascend the stairs, then silence, then the creak of the door, then the click of the latch. You remind your parents to ask for one mushroom pizza, because your sister loves mushroom pizza, and then run upstairs yourself. You proceed down the hall to the door of your sister's room. You hear music blaring from within the room. You also smell a strange odor. And you hear the fan running, which you find odd during this month of December. You open the door and peak into your sister's room. She and her friends are sitting on the floor, talking about the upcoming winter recess, smoking cigarettes. Your sister looks quickly in your direction. She obviously didn't expect you to come into the room. She jumps up from the floor, walks over to you, bends down, and grabs you gently by the shoulders. She pleads with you not to tell your parents about her smoking. You assure her that you'll never tell. After declaring you as the best sister ever, she turns back to her friends, grabbing a can of air freshener and spraying her room with the smell of summer peaches to eliminate the smell of cigarette smoke. One of her friends redirects the fan towards an open window. You leave your sister's room with the conviction never to tell on your sister.

This example illustrates the fact that a large number of youngsters who begin smoking live with smokers. When children have parents or siblings who smoke, they become more likely to start smoking, too. What better role model for a child than a parent or sibling? Here's a successful older sister who achieves excellent grades in school, excels in sports, and maintains a busy social life. She's admired by her friends and, more importantly, by your parents. Why wouldn't you aspire to grow up just like her? So you always study hard. You practice your lacrosse in the backyard. And now, you'll sneak your first cigarette from her dresser drawer when she's out with her friends.

So you see, as impressionable youngsters, we forge identities for ourselves based on how we wish to be perceived. We base this on experiences with friends, family, and society in general. As we live our daily lives, we pick characteristics that we find appealing, or interesting, or exciting in others. We even gather features from watching television and movies, picking apart the personalities of our favorite actors and actresses, or the characters they portray, and merging their characteristics with others we've chosen for ourselves. In this way, we piece together our individual identities, and fashion ourselves as we wish to be seen by society.

In this way, for whatever reason, you chose to portray yourself as a smoker. It may have been because your favorite actor in your favorite movie smoked. Or maybe the most popular girl in school, the prom queen, the captain of the soccer team, was a smoker. Or perhaps your older brother, the captain of the football team, the coolest guy you knew, was a smoker. In an attempt to create your own identity, you chose to emulate the smokers you encountered in your youth. You found them cool, or popular, or sophisticated. And there you stood, with your very first cigarette in one hand, and a book of matches in the other, prepared to install this new characteristic into your personality. You had chosen to become a smoker. And as you drew that first cigarette towards your lips, the defining moment in the birth of a smoker, how did you envision yourself? What were you thinking? Do you remember? Try to recollect your thoughts from the time you smoked that first cigarette; we'll be addressing them in a little while.

Did you enjoy your first cigarette?

There, you've done it. You've drawn your first cigarette to your lips and inhaled your first puff. You've become a smoker, right there in your sister's room, or in that alley behind the video arcade, or wherever you were at the time; you might not even remember. So, how did you feel? There are two aspects to answering this question correctly, physical and emotional. Chances are, within these two contexts, your answers are completely different.

Physically, you probably felt lousy. Typically one's first experience with a cigarette is memorable for its repulsiveness. Did you cough uncontrollably? Did you gag so much that you couldn't breathe? Were you coughing so much that you were doubled-over and drenched with sweat? People experience similar symptoms when they breathe in some environmental irritant, such as exhaust fumes or smoke from a fire, or from certain medical conditions, such as pneumonia or sinusitis. These are horrible symptoms that people usually try to avoid at all costs. They run away from the smoke. They take antibiotics and decongestants. They do everything possible to minimize or eliminate these symptoms. And they would never choose to suffer from them again. How many times do you see people running towards a burning building? Firefighters notwithstanding, people know that they'll suffer from terrible symptoms if they breathe in that smoke, and will run away from it. And even the firefighters wear protective masks to avoid breathing in the smoke. Logic would dictate, then, that given the repulsion of that first puff, you would throw away that first cigarette and avoid smoking at all costs.

So, then, why did you take that second puff from that first cigarette? Why did you run toward the burning building? If the initial experience was so unpleasant, why did you choose to suffer once again? Answering this question brings us to the difference between the physical experience and the emotional experience inherent in that first cigarette. Despite the physical discomfort, you emotionally felt great. Remember, you regarded smoking as a desirable quality. You wanted to be a smoker, and to enjoy the perks of a smoker's life. You wanted the popularity, and the success, and the maturity, and the sophistication. Before you ever took this first puff, you'd pictured yourself as a smoker, surrounded by friends, successful in life, throwing the touchdown pass, scoring another A+ in Social Studies, wearing the coolest clothes, being elected Class President, riding a horse into the sunset, beating the villain, preventing nuclear war, playing guitar on stage with the band. Well, after that first puff, you made yourself a smoker, and you were ready to reap the glory you perceived in a smoker's life. That was your transition period. That first puff was your defining moment. That's why you ran back into the burning building; your popularity, success, maturity, and sophistication were in that burning building and you were willing to suffer physically to achieve them. You felt physically ill but emotionally glorified.

Besides, the physical suffering doesn't last forever. After all, once you got used to inhaling the smoke, you wouldn't cough anymore, right? You never saw your friends, parents, brother, or sister cough, and they smoked all the time. So you were willing to endure short-term physical discomfort in order to achieve long-term emotional comfort. In this way, deciding to start smoking was just like any other personality-defining decision you made. For example, when you had your ears pierced, did it hurt? Sure it hurt, but it doesn't hurt anymore. And you loved showing up to school the following day with your new earrings. When you first learned to ride a skateboard, did it hurt? Sure it hurt; you had scuffs all over yourself to prove that it hurt. But it doesn't hurt anymore. And you loved the looks of admiration you'd elicit when you perform stunts in front of your friends. Did it hurt when you learned to swim? Sure it hurt; you almost drowned four times. But it doesn't hurt anymore. And you love watching your parents smile as you place yet another trophy on your shelf. The short-term pain led to long-term happiness. So sure it hurt when you started smoking. But it doesn't hurt anymore. And you love being a smoker.

So to answer this question, overall, you probably enjoyed that first cigarette tremendously, because it brought you closer to the person you wished to be at the time. In your quest to find your place in society, to define your individual personality, you decided to become a smoker. Sure, you decided to become other things, too; maybe you chose to be a soccer player, inline skater, choir singer, or chess club member. Maybe you wore ripped jeans, baseball caps, unlaced sneakers, or bandanas. But think about this for a moment. Do you still wear ripped jeans? Are you still a member of that chess club? Do you still don a bandana? Chances are you've left most of these characteristics behind, in your youth, the time in which they were important to you. So why, then, are you still smoking cigarettes?

How did you evolve as a smoker?

So now you've defined yourself; you've created your own individual identity. You were in your teens, maybe even younger, and you were happy with the personality you'd created for yourself. You were a jock, a loner, a nerd, a leader, a follower, whatever. And, you were a smoker. But thinking back to the person you were back then, are you the same person today? Does that identity still apply to you? Chances are, as a person, aside from being a smoker, you're much different from that person you created years ago.

The priorities of a youngster are much different from those of an adult and, therefore, the characteristics of importance must necessarily be different, too. We've described some of the important aspects of the life of a teenager. Showing up at school with newly-pierced ears. Whizzing past your classmates on your new skateboard. Hanging out with your big sister and her friends, listening to records. And, of course, cigarette smoking. However, as we grow towards adulthood, our priorities change and, therefore, our issues of importance likewise change. It no longer serves our best interest to be a great skateboarder, or a video game champ. You place your skateboard into storage, and drive away in your new car. You hang out less with your big sister listening to records, and more with your Guidance Counselor choosing colleges. And you realize that your membership in the chess club won't help you pay the bills.

And so you grow into an adult. You open bank accounts, buy cars, attend college, search for a job, wear suits, start families, and eventually grow old and retire. Along the way, you throw out your ripped jeans and bandanas, and put your baseball caps in the closet. You have to. On the one hand, you must portray yourself as an adult in order to achieve success in the world of adults. How would you look showing up for a college interview wearing a bandana on your head and unlaced sneakers on your feet? And when you interview with the CEO for that excellent job opportunity, would the CEO necessarily care that you're a great inline skater? And would you dare showing up on your wedding day wearing a baseball cap? These vestiges of childhood glory must necessarily be abandoned so that you may appropriately grow as an adult, and advance your role in society. No longer are you a skateboarder, video game champion, and grunge rocker. Now, you're a homeowner, parent, and wage earner. You no longer dress for popularity, or for attention, or for shock value. Now, you dress to land a job, to find a mate, and to set a good example for your children. You trade your ripped jeans, concert T-shirts, and baseball caps for power suits, blouses, and neckties. In your progression to adulthood, you change your garb to reflect your new set of obligations.

On the other hand, you're a little older now, and health concerns have become important. People state that children often seem invincible; or they just think they are. They ski down perilous slopes. They drive too fast. They come home in the wee hours of the morning after a night of partying. They eat fast food almost every day. And they sit in front of that television for hours. They give no thought as to the potential health outcomes of their behaviors. They're too young to understand that life is finite. But you're a responsible adult now, and you need to mind your health. You may hurt yourself skiing that steep hill; then you wouldn't be able to provide for your family. And you may get into a car accident if you don't obey the speed limit. You rarely stay up past midnight; you're usually asleep by ten o'clock. You eat less fast food, because you need to watch out for your cholesterol. And you watch less television, choosing to spend more time walking on your treadmill. You're mindful of life expectancy, and you choose to act responsibly in matters of health.

So, you see, you've actually evolved a great deal since your youth. Wherein you used to be carefree and flippant, you're now cautious and intelligent. You care more about financial security. You're gainfully employed. You're responsible for feeding, clothing, and sheltering others. You eat right and exercise. You've cast away your childhood self in exchange for your current, adult persona.

So, then, why do you still smoke? Why have you held onto this last vestige of your childhood? You were able to give up many things in your evolution to adulthood, some of which you enjoyed, and some of which even defined you as a person. So why didn't you give up cigarettes?

Why are you still smoking?

The creation of an individual adult identity is much like that for a youngster, which we have discussed previously. However, the driving forces are different, and therefore, the resultant list of desirable characteristics must necessarily differ. Adults need to support a family, hold a job, and stay healthy. Hence, it becomes "cool" to wear suits, join health clubs, eat nutritious foods, and buy homes. Adults wear scarves and hats in the winter and sun block in the summer. Adults drive minivans. Adults buy furniture. Adults make choices based on responsibility, not on popularity; on future success, not on present gratification.

So, then, why are you still smoking? What purpose does cigarette smoking serve in your adult life? If you were unable to leave cigarette smoking in your past, along with the rest of your childhood characteristics, then it must hold some value to your adult life as well, right? You must still receive some benefit from smoking.

Let's address this for a moment by reviewing a few examples; see how realistic they seem to you. First, we'll see if cigarette smoking will help you land a job. There you stand, outside the large wooden door that leads to the office of the CEO of the company for which you wish to work. Your shirt is ironed, your suit is crisp, and your portfolio is tucked tightly under your arm. You hear your name called, and you turn to your right to see a secretary pointing to the door. She states that the CEO will see you now. With guarded confidence, you turn the doorknob and pull, and then stride through the open door. Across the room sits the CEO. She stands to greet you, and then offers you a seat at her desk. You feel nervous, but positive; you've prepared for this interview for weeks.

The interview begins. She fires questions at you, and you field them swiftly. She requests your qualifications, and you present four glowing letters of recommendation from your portfolio. She demands samples of your work, and you submit to her some of your best. As the interview progresses, you become more relaxed and confident. You have this job locked.

The CEO pushes out from behind her desk and stands, extending her hand to you. You, likewise, stand and shake her hand. She then states that, unfortunately, you will not get the job. Disconcerted, you labor for one last effort that would change her mind. Suddenly hopeful, you reach into your pocket for your cigarettes and matches. You pull out one cigarette, light up, and sit back down into your chair. Seeing you smoking in her office, the CEO smiles and apologizes. She didn't realize that you're a smoker. You refer her to page four of your resume, just after your list of awards, to the chronological account of your smoking history.

She's elated. Of course you're hired. In fact, you'd make a perfect vice president. She reaches into her desk, pulls out a cigarette, lights up, and laughs with you over the entire misunderstanding.

Does this seem possible? The fact is, your cigarette smoking would not help you land a job. Smoking does not bolster your resume, or make you a more desirable candidate, all other things being equal. As a matter of fact, many workplaces are becoming smoke-free in response to local legislation preventing smoking at the workplace, in recognition of the health dangers of second-hand smoke. We conclude that cigarette smoking does not help an adult land a job.

As another example, how about we discuss buying a home. You walk up the front walk with your family towards a beautiful brick house, noticing the lush front lawn and manicured landscaping. As you approach the front steps, the door to the house swings open. You recognize your realtor standing in the entrance foyer; he invites you into the house. He guides you through the entrance foyer, past the spiral staircase, and into the living room. As you tour the house, you count four fireplaces, five bathrooms, and five bedrooms. As you pass through the dining room, you peer out the back window to the expansive backyard. This is the perfect home for you and your family.

You and your family sit with the realtor at the dining room table, and express your interest in buying the house. Your realtor quotes an asking price of $500,000. That's much more than you expected to pay. You offer $450,000, but the realtor states that the owners of the house are firm on their asking price. Perturbed, you reach into your pocket, and pull out a cigarette. Your realtor, seeing you smoking, produces a wide grin. He reveals to you that the asking price of $500,000 is for non-smokers. Anyone who smokes can have the house for only $100,000. Elated, you commit to the purchase of your new home.

This doesn't seem too realistic, does it? Cigarette smoking wouldn't help an adult purchase a home either. We can repeat this exercise for all of the obligations that adults maintain. Cigarette smoking will not help you land a job, buy a home, raise a family, purchase a car, type a resume, go to PTA meetings, buy a suit, shop for food, or furnish a house. You'd be hard pressed to find anything in your adult life that requires you to smoke cigarettes. Cigarette smoking serves no useful purpose in your adult life. Non-smokers can buy homes, raise families, and shop for food just as well as smokers. In fact, as we'll discuss in a later chapter, smoking is only harmful to your health and the health of those around you. So why are you still smoking?

Summary

As you mature from childhood to adulthood, you forge identities for yourself based on each stage of growth. When you're young, superficial and materialistic items, such as clothes and music, carry great import in the creation of your identity. Cigarettes carry weight during this time, making you feel popular, or sophisticated, or mature, or rebellious. As you age, you abandon such superficial elements and adopt more meaningful pursuits, such as matters of family, employment, and health. In this stage, cigarettes have no clear role and, in fact, may actually be detrimental to these pursuits. However, you simply continue to smoke. Hopefully you now see how superfluous cigarettes are in your life, how they offer no benefit to your life right now. There is truly no rational benefit that an adult derives from smoking cigarettes.

So why do you smoke? You smoke because you're addicted to smoking. That's all. That's the answer to the question. You smoke because your addiction to cigarettes supercedes rational thought about its lack of benefit. You know now that smoking cigarettes offers you no true advantage in your daily life. You also know the health risks of smoking. Cigarette smoking is a pure negative-nothing good, all bad. Yet, you continue to smoke. You refuse to remove this pure negative from your life. Why would you want to continue exposing yourself to such malignance? What would you say if I asked you to jump out of a window? There's no benefit to jumping out a window. And you stand to hurt yourself greatly. Nothing good, all bad. Of course you wouldn't just jump out that window if I asked you to. But if I asked you to smoke a cigarette, would you? It's the same scenario; nothing good, all bad.

Now do you understand why you smoke? Or more importantly, do you understand why you shouldn't be smoking anymore? Why you don't need to smoke anymore? How cigarette smoking only harms you, without offering you any benefit for your current life? Recognize cigarette smoking as an unessential evil instead of a necessity, as an addiction instead of a choice, as a remnant of the past instead of a requirement for the present, and you'll be ready to quit for good.

Why's Smoking So Bad?

In order to understand why you need to quit smoking, you first need to understand why cigarette smoking is so bad for you. In order to understand this, however, you need to think a long time into your future. While cigarette smoking is associated with a great number of health concerns, you're likely experiencing none of them right now. Sure, you may get winded after you run up a flight of stairs. You may cough every once in a while. But you're probably not dealing with any of the major health issues for which cigarettes can be responsible. That's because the risks associated with smoking cigarettes increase with time, meaning that the longer you smoke, the more of an issue they become. To phrase that in a more foreboding way, while you may not be overtly aware of these issues in the course of your daily life, they may be building up slowly inside of you, escaping your detection, waiting to show themselves twenty or thirty years from now. But since they're not bothering you now, why should you worry about them now, right? Live for the here and now. Live for today. Worry about the future in the future.

Well, in this chapter, I will show you absolutely why you need to worry about them now by delivering you to your future. What I am going to do is reveal to you your future as a smoker. Rather than nag you about the ills of smoking and hope you listen to me, I will show you how severely cigarette-related health issues can affect you later in life. Again, by helping you to understand how smoking will impact you later in life, I'm hoping you will come to your own realization about needing to stop smoking right now, and not waiting for the future. Since the effects of smoking depend on the passage of time, the sooner you quit the better. You want to stop smoking before these health concerns become real for you. By stopping now, you'll minimize your chance of developing these problems, and you'll enjoy a longer, healthier life.

Before we begin this exercise in imagination, I want you to do a little math for me. Count the number of cigarettes you smoke in a day. Now, break out your calculator and multiply this number by 365, the number of days in a year (we'll ignore leap years). Now multiply this number by the number of years you've been smoking. For example, if you smoke forty cigarettes (two packs) per day, and you've smoked for ten years, then 40 times 365 times 10 equal 146,000 cigarettes. Wow, that's a lot.

Now, take your total and multiply by seven. So for our example, 146,000 times 7 equals 1,022,000. What does this number mean? This is the number of minutes of life you've lost by smoking cigarettes! For each cigarette you smoke, you shorten your life by seven minutes. In our example, our smoker has shortened his or her life by over one million minutes. To figure this out in years of life lost, divide your total number of minutes by 525,600, which is the number of minutes in a year. Our example smoker has lost almost two years of life by smoking for only ten years! And if our example continues to smoke, he or she will continue to lose seven minutes of life for each cigarette smoked.

By this calculation, if you smoke two packs per day, you shorten your life by almost five hours each day. Think of all the things you can do in five hours. Weddings can last five hours. Sporting events can last five hours. First dates can last five hours. How about a New Year's Eve party, or your parents' Anniversary Party, or a loved one's surgical procedure? Are these things less important to you than cigarettes? Are you willing to sacrifice any of these things for one day of smoking? Wouldn't you like to be around for these events? I hope this math exercise began to put cigarette smoking into perspective for you. Cigarette smoking really does kill.

One more task before we begin. I want you to try to guess how many cigarettes you need to smoke in order to suffer ill health effects from smoking. Plenty of smokers attempt to justify their smoking behavior by proclaiming that they only smoke a certain number of cigarettes per day. But how many cigarettes can you actually get away with smoking without negatively impacting your health? Ten? Six? Two?

How about none. That's right. The fact is that smoking as little as one cigarette per day can cause ill health effects. And every individual additional cigarette you smoke only serves to magnify your risk of adverse health consequences. A perfect medical example of this fact is emphysema. Recent research in emphysema suggests that cigarette smoking causes emphysema by triggering an inborn predisposition to develop the condition; once this predisposition is activated, you don't necessarily need to keep smoking for emphysema to develop. This is akin to pulling a trigger and causing a bullet to be shot from a gun; once you pull the trigger, you launch the bullet, and you don't need to keep pulling the trigger to make the bullet fly. Likewise, once you start smoking, you may not necessarily need to keep smoking in order to develop emphysema. Theoretically speaking, you may only need to smoke one cigarette in your lifetime to give yourself emphysema. Now I didn't share this fact with you to get you depressed; truly, only about fifteen percent of smokers will develop emphysema, anyway. But I wanted to illustrate to you that cutting down on your smoking will not help you. You can't just reduce your cigarette smoking; you need to quit.

Next, I'll help you to picture yourself as being inflicted with various smoking-related illnesses. I'm not doing this to be morbid, mind you; I need you to understand what you'll be doing to yourself if you continue to smoke. While you may feel fine today, your future quality of life will be dramatically altered by smoking. Turn on your imagination, and read on.

Emphysema

You wake up on a cold Sunday morning. Actually, you were up most of the night, anyway. Just like every night, you were up most of the night coughing. You can't remember the last time you had a good night's sleep. You usually wake up eight or nine times every night coughing. Sometimes you wake up gasping for air because the tube in your nose that gives you extra oxygen falls out. You feel so tired all the time, but you find it impossible to get even one good night's sleep.

You sit up at the edge of your bed and adjust your oxygen tube. You check the meter on your oxygen tank, making sure you'll have enough to last you the day. You remember that your friends are coming over today, and you usually talk for hours about the good ol' days. You listen, mostly; whenever you speak for more than a minute straight, you have to stop to catch your breath. You sit back on the edge of the bed, thinking back to when you were younger, when you used to bound up flights of stairs without getting winded. Now, you can barely talk without losing your breath.

You stand up from the bed, grab the handle on your oxygen tank, and start walking toward the bathroom. Your bathroom is down the hall from your bedroom, maybe twenty feet from your bed. On a good day, it takes you about five minutes to make the walk. You stop every few feet to catch your breath. Even with the oxygen, every step is a struggle.

As you walk, you hold onto your armchair, the wall, the table in the hallway, anything you can grab to remove the burden that you have become to your own feet. The steroids you've taken for the past five years have stricken you with myopathy, a horrible muscular weakness that makes it difficult to walk, especially up a flight of stairs or across long distances. That's why, for all intents and purposes, you live in your bedroom upstairs. If you tried to venture down to the kitchen, you'd need to be carried back upstairs.

You return to your bedroom-another five minute struggle from the bathroom-and sink back into your bed. After you catch your breath, you reach for the remote and turn on the television. After you catch your breath again, you look up at the TV and realize once again that you don't care for Sunday television programming. You enjoy much more the programs that are on during the week. The poor condition of your lungs prevents you from holding a job. You sit in your bed and watch television every day of your life. That's your life. Your whole life.

It's midday, and the doorbell rings. Your friends have come over. As you struggle from the bed, you think about the journey ahead of you-out of the bedroom, across the hall, down the stairs, and through the foyer to the front door. You're thankful your friends are patient individuals. You grab your oxygen tank and begin the ten minute trip downstairs. As you clamber down the stairs, you imagine what your friends must be thinking of you in your current state. You remember how many times they tried to get you to stop smoking. They all stopped when they were in their thirties; you were the only one who didn't. Your younger brother smoked, and he pressured you to keep smoking with him. He died a few years ago.

You finally make it to the front door. You peer out the window to confirm it's your friends. You see your four pals standing on your front porch in their sweat suits. They must have just come from playing racquetball. You remember again, they stopped smoking a long time ago.

As you open the door on this cold winter afternoon, a gush of wind rushes into your house. You take in a deep breath of cold December air. This was a big mistake. You suddenly become very short of breath. Your friends look at you with concerned faces, and tell you you're starting to turn blue. You stumble to the side, knocking over your oxygen tank. As you fall to the floor, gasping for air, you think how thankful you are that your friends are there with you; they can take you to the Emergency Room.

Heart Disease

You're lying on a narrow metal table in a large, cold room on the eighth floor of your community hospital. You're in a thin hospital gown, and your clothes are in a plastic bag on the floor beneath you. There's a large needle sticking into your right leg, through which your heart doctor has snaked a long catheter. He's injecting dye into the arteries in your heart. You're watching everything on the monitors above your head.

You drift away, and think back to what happened two days ago. You had just eaten breakfast. It was your 52nd birthday, and your spouse had made you a delicious breakfast of pancakes and eggs, which you enjoyed very much. You went to the refrigerator, grabbed a pitcher, and poured yourself a tall glass of water. With water in hand, you reached into the cabinet over the sink and pulled out a basket of bottles. These bottles contain your medications, which you need to take several times each day. Every day. You're used to the routine by now; you've been taking all these pills for the past ten years. You sat back down at the table and began opening one bottle at a time, removing one pill from each. It's a pretty arduous task when you have eleven different bottles of pills. It's easier at night; you only have to take nine pills then.

After you swallowed your medication, you got up and walked to the front door to get the newspaper. You opened the door and looked out to see the newspaper by the curb on your front walk. You put on your slippers and walked down your front walk. As you bent over to pick up the newspaper, you felt a strong weight suddenly fill your chest. It was one of the worst pains you ever felt in your life. You called out to your spouse to call an ambulance. Fearing the worst, you remember your doctor telling you that this might happen if you kept smoking.

The ambulance arrived at your front walk in about ten minutes. The EMS workers rushed to your side and laid you down on your front lawn. There, they put an oxygen mask on your face, and started two IV lines in your arms. As your neighbors began to gather, the EMS workers then stuck a series of metal leads to your chest. They attached wires to these leads, then asked you to lie perfectly still. As you quietly stared up at the cloudy sky, you noticed a cold sweat arise over your forehead. One of the EMS workers broke the silence, shouting to the others that you were having an "M.I." and that they needed to rush you to the hospital. As they lifted you onto a stretcher, you wondered to yourself what those letters stood for. Your question was answered as the EMS workers lifted you into the ambulance; you overheard one of your neighbors telling your worried spouse that an "M.I." is a heart attack. He learned this after his wife died from a heart attack last year.

A tap on your shoulder brings you back to the hospital room. Your heart doctor wants to show you something on the monitor. As you watch, he injects dye into the catheter in your leg; you feel a warm sensation ascend your leg as he pushes the plunger. On the monitor, you observe a thick line of white that abruptly shrinks to a thin string. Your heart doctor points out that the thin string you see is an area of blockage in one of the arteries supplying your heart. Not bad, you surmise; you must have more arteries to feed your heart. Then, your heart doctor points out a second, third, and fourth thin string.

You're wheeled into the recovery area of the Cardiology laboratory. As you lie flat on the stretcher, you feel another tap on your shoulder. You look up to see your heart doctor standing over you with another individual. This other person is obviously also a doctor, but you've never seen him before. He's wearing a pair of green scrubs under a crisp white lab coat. He's looking at your chart. Your heart doctor introduces you to him; he's a heart surgeon. Unfortunately, since four of the arteries in your heart have blockages, you're going to need open-heart surgery. Right now.

You're wheeled down the hall to the pre-surgical area. Here, your family is allowed to come to see you for a few minutes. They wish you luck, and are then escorted to the waiting room. As you watch them being led away, you think back to their efforts to get you to stop smoking. Your children used to plead with you to stop; they learned in health class how bad smoking can be for you, and since then tried everything to get you to quit. As they turn the corner, you start to wonder if you'll ever see them again.

Lung Cancer

You're sitting in the passenger seat of your car, being driven to your doctor's office. Trying to look at the parked cars as you ride by them only makes your nausea that much worse. Besides that, the bright sun is making your headaches even worse than usual. You've been feeling so sick that you haven't had a decent meal in two weeks. All you can eat is soup and bread; anything heavier makes you vomit. You know the doctor's going to scold you for not eating, too. She's told you throughout, since the day you were diagnosed with lung cancer, that you have to eat to keep your weight up. Since that day, you've lost sixty-five pounds. That was two months ago.

You pull into the doctor's parking lot. You adjust your hat, still self-conscious that your treatments caused you to lose your hair. After checking yourself in the mirror, you open the car door and stand up. You walk around to the back of the car and open the trunk. You're in excruciating pain. You have lesions in your spine that cause so much pain that you can barely walk without a thick fiberglass brace, which is in your trunk. You reach down, pick up your brace, and put in on. This reduces your pain from debilitating to merely intolerable.

You walk into the lobby of your doctor's building. The security guard asks you for which suite you're looking. You look right back at him and honestly cannot remember. You turn to the building's directory, which lists all the doctors along with their suite number. Now, what is your doctor's name again? None of these look familiar. You struggle to remember your doctor's name. Luckily, someone you think you recognize approaches you. Turns out it's your doctor, returning from down the hall. She grabs you by the arm and escorts you to her office.

In the examining room, you tell your doctor about how sick you've felt. She fears that the eight lesions in your brain are causing swelling, causing your head-aches and forgetfulness. She reminds you that the only way you can really treat these is with radiation therapy to your entire brain. You smirk, remembering that when you started radiation therapy, you only had two lesions in your brain. That was last month.

She decides to give you more steroids, which she hopes will reduce the swell-ing in your brain. Unfortunately, you think, they also give you those fungal infec-tions in your throat that make it painful to swallow. She also writes you a new prescription for morphine, for which you are very thankful. You needed an extra dose of morphine to reduce your pain enough just to get yourself to her office today.

She then hands you a brochure, and tells you to read it at your leisure and let her know what you think. As you leave her office, you open the brochure and begin to read. You see that this is a pamphlet for something called "Hospice Care." Curious, you sit on a nearby bench in the lobby and begin to read. You come to learn that this is a brochure for a program that specializes in end-of-life care. You peruse passages on how to prepare yourself and your family for your death. Feeling a little nervous after reading this pamphlet, you reach into your pocket, pull out a cigarette, sit back on the bench and smoke. You laugh to your-self, remembering how your family yelled at you just yesterday for not being able to stop smoking even after you were diagnosed with lung cancer. But you know better. Even your doctor told you that you might as well keep smoking. Because whether you smoke or not at this point, you only have three months to live.

Vascular Disease

You wake up on a Monday morning, enthusiastic about what this day holds for you. Today is your first appointment for physical therapy since your surgery. You were in the hospital for two weeks, and then have been confined to bed at home for the past six weeks. You were allowed to do exercises in bed, but you haven't been allowed to get out of bed. Today will be the first day.

As you get dressed for your appointment, you think back to the long road that brought you to this point. A few months ago, you noticed that the top of your right foot began to hurt. For several months before that, your legs would hurt when you walked for a few minutes. You'd need to stop walking and sit down to make the pain go away. But at this point, the pain moved to the top of your foot and didn't go away, no matter what you did. Also, you noticed that some of the toes on your right foot seemed to be turning blue.

Concerned, you decided to go to your doctor, who sent you for a battery of tests. He concluded that because of your smoking, the blood flow to your right leg has become severely impaired, and that you needed to be seen by a surgeon. Although he looked worried, he stated that sometimes Vascular Surgeons can open up the blood vessels in the leg with a catheter and balloon, or they can bypass the arteries with a graft to restore blood flow past the blockage, just like avoiding a traffic jam.

You went to the surgeon the following week. After examining you, he scheduled you for an angiogram at the hospital. He told you that he would need to stick a needle into the artery in your right leg, and then inject dye into the artery to assess the extent of blockage. You expected this; your regular doctor told you about this. You just didn't expect it to happen so soon; the surgeon scheduled you for that afternoon.

You arrived at the hospital, proceeded to the Radiology Department, signed in, and waited anxiously in the waiting room, remembering the concerned look on your doctor's face as he referred you to the surgeon. After a few minutes, you heard your name called, and an assistant led you to the angiogram area. There, your surgeon was waiting for you. There was also an anesthesiologist who would give you medication to sleep during the procedure. The surgeon told you that depending on what they found, they may need to take you to surgery right after the angiogram. You felt a medication being injected into your arm, then you fell fast asleep.

The next thing you remembered was waking up in the recovery room, feeling a strange pain in your right leg. You overheard someone at the foot of your bed telling someone else that you weighed 150 pounds. Funny, you thought; when you weighed yourself yesterday you were 185 pounds.

The doorbell rings, returning you from your remembrances. Fully dressed by now, you shift to the edge of your bed, where your wheelchair awaits. You slide into your wheelchair, unlock the wheels, and push off towards the front door. As you open the door, you see your physical therapist on the porch, holding a large bag. Reaching into the bag, he pulls out a three foot long metal rod with a strap and plastic receptacle at one end, and a white tube sock and sneaker at the other. You recognize it as the artificial leg you chose from the catalog two weeks ago. You enthusiastically welcome your physical therapist into your home; today will be the first day you'll try to walk since your right leg was amputated.

Burns

You awaken from what seemed like a deep sleep to find yourself lying on your back, yet you feel like you're moving very quickly. As you come to, you realize you're in an ambulance. You hear sirens blaring, and you notice two EMS workers by your feet. You try to speak, but as the first word comes out, you start to cough uncontrollably. As you cough, black smoke begins to fill the ambulance. Noticing this, one of the EMS workers leans toward your head, pushes you back onto the stretcher, and replaces an oxygen mask onto your face. After instructing you to relax and take long deep breaths, he returns to wrapping your feet.

As you awaken more, you begin to remember the events leading you to this point. You had just finished breakfast on this sunny Sunday morning, and after you cleaned your dishes, you walked out onto your front porch to read the newspaper and enjoy a cigarette. You leaned back into the cushion on your new wicker sofa, placed the newspaper and your glass of orange juice next to the ashtray on the table, lit up your cigarette, and soaked up the morning sun. After a few puffs, you placed your cigarette on the table and picked up the newspaper. Nestled in your new comfortable sofa, reading the headlines, you began to feel sleepy. You decided to close your eyes for a short nap.

You awoke several minutes later feeling much warmer than you did before you nodded off. You also noticed a strange smell, like something was burning in an oven. Curious as to which of your neighbors burned their lunch, you opened your eyes to look around. You were shocked to see a wall of smoke and flames in front of you on the porch. Although you couldn't see them, you heard people screaming on your front lawn. As you gasped in horror, you inhaled a large amount of thick, black smoke, and felt a sudden strong warmth enter your chest. Coughing incessantly, you leapt from the sofa and began feeling for your front door; you couldn't see anything, having been enveloped in smoke. You've never been so frightened in your entire life.

You finally found the front door. You reached for the doorknob, hoping you could escape the flames and smoke inside your house. As you turned the knob, your hand was singed by its heat. You opened the door to find your home engulfed in flames and smoke, just like your porch. Not knowing in which direction to walk, you decided to try to find your telephone so you could call for help. You dropped to the floor, remembering the lessons about fires you were taught in elementary school. You crawled through the living room to the kitchen. You stood up, reached for the phone, and dialed 911. Becoming lightheaded, you dictated your address to the dispatcher on the telephone. You began to feel severe pains all over your body. The last thing you remembered was falling to the floor.

Feeling a sharp stick in your right hand, you return from your thoughts. An EMS worker was trying to start a second IV line in your hand. You look to see your entire right arm wrapped in gauze. In fact, both of your arms and legs, as well as your chest, are wrapped up in several layers of gauze and covered with cream. The EMS worker asks you if you're in pain. Wondering why you wouldn't be in pain, you state that you're not. Sensing your confusion, the EMS worker tells you that you're probably not feeling any pain because you suffered a third degree burn, which usually fries the nerve endings in your skin. He says you're better off this way, because you'll need to be re-wrapped in gauze three or four times every day, and this process typically causes excruciating pain.

You feel the ambulance come to a stop. The back doors of the ambulance open, and several people in scrubs and white coats grab your stretcher and pull you out. From the ambulance bay, you're wheeled into the hospital, down a long hallway, and into the intensive care unit. You're lifted from the stretcher onto a bed, and a curtain is drawn around you. There, your clothes, covered with soot, are exchanged for a gown. You open the curtain to see a physician standing in wait. He's holding several packets of gauze in his arms. He introduces himself as a burn specialist, and states he needs to get to know you better, since you and he will likely be spending a few months together.

Summary

The fact is, cigarette smoking is implicated in many medical conditions, including heart disease, vascular disease, diabetes, rheumatoid arthritis, cataracts, and duodenal ulcers. As far as cancer is concerned, smoking can be responsible for cancers of the lung, pancreas, colon, ovary, kidney, and esophagus. These are all serious medical conditions that will ruin your quality of life as you age. In fact, they may not even allow you to age; you may just die several years prematurely because of your habit.

Keep in mind the examples we reviewed in this chapter the next time you reach for a cigarette. I hope they helped you to understand how cigarette smoking can impact your future health. Imagine not being able to walk across your own house because you can't breathe. Imagine being told that you needed to have one of your legs amputated. Cigarettes make you feel great when you're young and healthy, but they'll cause you sickness and disability during your later years.

There are horrible things in cigarettes. Things you would never think of inhaling voluntarily. About four thousand things, actually. There's formaldehyde in cigarettes. Formaldehyde is commonly found in paints, glues, and resins. It is also the preservative used in funeral homes. There's citronella in cigarettes. Citronella is that stuff you burn in candles to keep insects away. There's radium in cigarettes. Radium is a radioactive substance that was once used to make glow-in-the-dark watches glow. There's tar in cigarettes. We use tar on our roofs, and on city streets. In cigarettes, tar is a definite carcinogen.

So, stop smoking now, and enjoy a healthier future. More importantly, stop smoking now and be alive in the future.

Addiction Or Habit?

You've been smoking for quite a while now. Is it just that you're used to smoking, or are you unable to stop? In other words, is smoking your habit or your addiction? When trying to stop smoking, this is an important distinction to make. You know that you need to stop smoking, whether you are an habitual or addicted smoker. We've already determined that. But figuring out whether you're a habitual or addicted smoker will help you gauge the difficulty you'll have stopping. Not that stopping smoking is ever easy, mind you. It's just that if you're addicted, you'll need to expend a greater effort to quit than if you just smoke out of habit. So, ascertaining if you're truly addicted will allow you to better prepare yourself for the intense challenge at hand. Conversely, if you decide that you merely smoke out of habit, then you verily have no reason to keep smoking, and you should find it relatively simple to quit.

First, we need to define the terms so you understand the differences between a habit and an addiction. Then, we'll determine whether your smoking behavior is habitual or addictive. Finally, we'll discuss some methods to conquer the addiction you likely possess.

Habit

A habit is something you do that has become a part of your regular routine. Habits can be healthy or unhealthy, and can be significant or insignificant. You may not even be consciously aware of some of the things you do habitually. In fact, as a lesson to yourself, I would encourage you to count how many things you do habitually in the course of a day; you can't imagine how long this list may become. I'll start you off with an example of some morning habits. Say you wake up at six o'clock in the morning. That's habit number one. You roll over and hit the snooze button to give yourself seven more minutes of rest. That's habit number two. Seven minutes after six, you get out of bed. Habit number three. You walk to the kitchen and set up a pot of coffee to brew. Number four. Next, you jump into the shower to wash up, then you get dressed, and then go back to the kitchen for breakfast. Numbers five, six, and seven. If you wait until after breakfast to put your shoes on, that's number eight. After you put your shoes on, you walk back to the kitchen to pour yourself a cup of coffee. Number nine. You drink one cup of coffee, then pour the rest into a thermal cup to bring with you to work. Number ten.

That's ten habits, and you haven't even left the house. As you can see from this example, habits are not necessarily bad things. Habits are just patterns of behavior that you've developed over time, and that you've become used to as part of your regular routine, your daily rituals, so to speak. So then, how does cigarette smoking become a habit? Actually, cigarette smoking can easily become a part of your regular routine, one of your daily rituals. Think about this. Are there certain times during the day when you always smoke a cigarette, say, first thing in the morning, or after dinner, or when you have a cup of coffee, or while you're reading the newspaper? I'm sure there are several times every day when you smoke a cigarette, same time, same place, seemingly with no justification. Does smoking a cigarette make that cup of coffee taste better? Does smoking a cigarette help you digest your dinner? Does smoking a cigarette fill the newspaper with good news instead of bad? Of course not. The fact is, these are your habitual cigarettes. Smoking these cigarettes, for whatever reason, has become an expected, predictable part of your day. They've become a part of your daily rituals. So, every morning you open the front door, grab the newspaper, bring it into the kitchen, pour yourself a cup of coffee, sit down at the table, open to the Sports Section, and light up a cigarette. And every evening you finish your dinner, gather the dirty plates, carry them to the sink, walk to the den, and smoke a cigarette before rinsing off the dishes and placing them in the dishwasher. Smoking cigarettes has just become a thing you do. It's as simple as that.

But how, then, did cigarette smoking become so ingrained into your regular routine, such that it's now as automatic as washing your face in the morning and brushing your teeth at night? Probably just like any other thing you do habitually. You must have originally had some reasons for the things you now do habitually, otherwise you wouldn't have started doing them in the first place. For example, say you drive to work every day along the same side roads instead of taking the highway. Certainly you don't sit in your car every morning debating whether to take the side streets or the highway; taking the side streets has become your habit, your regular routine. But why did you initially start taking the side roads instead of the highway. Logic would dictate that a highway should be faster than the side roads. Maybe when you first started this job, you took the highway every morning, but eventually found that the traffic was too heavy. So you grabbed a map, seeking an alternative to the highway, and outlined a route taking the side roads. You tried this new route one day and found that you arrived at work twenty minutes earlier. Wonderful. You've taken this route every day since. Notice how this habit was borne out of an active decision you made.

Now, we need to figure out why you started smoking your habitual cigarettes. You must have had your reasons, right? Not necessarily good reasons, just reasons. Remember, there's really no good reason to start smoking cigarettes. Regardless, you must have made active decisions that allowed these cigarettes to become habitual for you. Say, for example, you and a friend of yours decided to start smoking together during high school. You met every day after school at the corner deli, where a group of your friends met for cigarettes and soda, and smoked a cigarette together before you went home, so your parents wouldn't find out. But what happened when you finished high school? No more covert meetings outside the deli. You went off to college, and your friend went elsewhere. But every day after classes, on the way back to your dorm, you would smoke a cigarette. You'd be sure to finish it before you arrived at the dorm, because your roommate didn't smoke. Pretty soon, you found a new group of friends who also smoked, and met with them at the Student Center after classes to smoke. Then what happened when you finished college? You got a job and joined the work force. No more smoking at the Student Center. But every day since then, on the way back home from work, while driving in your car, you've smoked a cigarette, all by yourself. And you have ever since, same time, every day.

So, back in high school you made an active decision to smoke a cigarette after school. You had your reasons at the time. For one, your parents wouldn't find out that you smoke, because you kept it out of your home. Second, you wanted to smoke with your friend, who also smoked at that time. Third, you knew that your other friends smoked there at that time, and you wanted to smoke with them to be cool. But, do any of these reasons apply now? You may not even live with your parents anymore, and you certainly don't have to answer to them at this point in your life. And you probably have a completely different group of friends with which you spend your time. In fact, your current friends may not even smoke. And besides, what purpose does smoking by yourself in your car every day serve? It certainly can't make you look cool; you're by yourself.

So then, why do you continue to smoke that particular cigarette every day on the way home from work, in your car, all by yourself? Force of habit. It's that simple. You're just used to it. Every day, same time, same place, one cigarette. You don't really have a good reason to smoke that cigarette anymore, but you still smoke it every day, habitually. Just like all the other cigarettes you smoke in the course of your day. Just like driving to work along the side streets every day, or hitting the snooze button every morning before getting out of bed, or drinking two cups of coffee every day with breakfast. The only problem is that these other habits aren't necessarily bad for you. Cigarette smoking, as a habit, is definitely bad for you.

You need to recognize and squelch habits which are bad, or maladaptive, or harmful. For instance, I would always wait for all of my monthly bills to arrive in the mail before sitting down with the checkbook and paying them. I originally began this pattern in college, while living in the dorms; because I was so busy attending classes, studying for tests, completing homework assignments, and frequenting parties, I developed this habit as a time-saving measure. I would sit down once each month with a pile of bills, write out a bunch of checks, and mail them all out in one shot. Done until next month. This became my habitual way of paying bills. The problem arose after I graduated from college. While furthering my education after college, I lived in apartments. The number of bills I had to pay doubled; and to make matters worse, my bills arrived at all different times of the month. All of a sudden, I was paying late charges every month because I would hold onto some bills past their due dates, just so I could pay all of my bills at the same time. Obviously, my habit had become maladaptive, in that I was losing money through late charges. My habit needed to be changed actively. Now that I'm a homeowner, I sit down weekly and pay bills. This is my new habitual way of paying the bills. Because of this change in my originally maladaptive habit, I avoid paying late charges.

Likewise, you need to actively stop your maladaptive, unhealthy smoking habit. Cigarette smoking no longer holds the benefits it once provided. The driving forces that brought you to begin smoking are long in your past, and have no effect on your daily life today. Cigarette smoking is a habit you absolutely need to break.

Addiction

Compared to a habit, an addiction is an entirely different entity; unfortunately, it's also a more ominous entity. Defining the term "addiction" is challenging because, for one, you can be addicted to just about anything. We will be discussing an addiction to cigarettes, but people can be addicted to television, exercise, slot machines, pornography, fruit, books or even other people. Also, people can be addicted on any of several levels; addictions can be physical, emotional, behavioral, or cognitive. Let's compare addictions to habits.

Imagine an addiction as a habit that has gone too far. We've discussed how habits become so ingrained into your daily routine that they become automatic behaviors. You perform habits without actual purposeful thought. Furthermore, you probably don't suffer any adverse consequences if you fail to perform your habit now and again. For example, do you truly suffer if you hit the snooze button one extra time and sleep an extra seven minutes in the morning? Unlikely. Now imagine if you were punished, in some way, every time you failed to perform your habit. Every time you skip a habitual act, you suffer. If this happens, then this habit has become an addiction. For example, take cigarettes. Say you decide to skip one cigarette during your day. What happens? Chances are you experience strong withdrawal symptoms. You suffer. Cigarette smoking has become an addiction, and the experience of withdrawal symptoms is your punishment for skipping that cigarette. The punishment comes from your brain, which wants nicotine and which tries to force you into smoking again through exacting on you withdrawal symptoms. Your habit has gone too far.

Imagine an addiction as a habit that doesn't make sense. Habits are usually productive behaviors that help you through your day. They can be time-saving, or money-saving, or comforting. Even if habits are maladaptive, they're typically not harmful or dangerous. A harmful or dangerous habit is called an addiction. Addictions don't make sense because it's nonsensical to repeat behaviors which are harmful or dangerous. Rather than prematurely belabor cigarettes as our example, let's talk about the Internet. The Internet, as we all know, is an invaluable tool, allowing us to research topics, communicate with friends and family, plan vacations, make purchases, and follow current events. Most of us have computers in our homes, and many of us surf the Internet every day, regularly, as a habit. You may use the computer in the morning while you eat breakfast, or during your lunch hour at work, or perhaps at night before retiring to bed. The Internet can help us save both time and money. However, does it make sense to leave your family sitting in another room while you stare at your computer for hours on end? Does it make sense to stay up so late at night surfing the Internet that you sleep through your alarm and arrive late for work in the morning? Does it make sense to spend so much time on the Internet that you miss meals and avoid socializing with your friends? Of course not. These are examples of addictive uses of the Internet, uses that don't make sense.

Imagine an addiction as a habit that ultimately leads to despair. Addictions are characterized universally by poor long-term outcomes. Exercising, as a habit, is wonderful over the long term. Exercising helps you lower your weight, increase your stamina and energy level, and control various medical conditions. Taking a multivitamin, as a habit, is also great. It helps you fill in deficiencies in vitamins and minerals that exist in your diet, assuring a healthy meal plan. Retiring to bed early at night, as a habit, is outstanding. It helps you to awaken refreshed and ready to start the day. On the other hand, drinking too much alcohol, as an addiction, is terrible. Excessive use of alcohol can lead to car accidents, seizures, liver failure, and cancer. Gambling, as an addiction, is likewise horrible. It results in the loss of your financial security, and possibly even your life savings. And yes, cigarette smoking, as an addiction, causes emphysema, cancer, heart disease, and countless other medical ills. Addictions lead to despair.

Imagine an addiction as a habit that is mandatory. Be them automatic or planned, habitual behaviors are ultimately voluntary. You're not forced to hit that snooze button in the morning by some undeniable force. Your car doesn't guide you away from the highway, through the side streets, against your will. Your clothes don't jump onto you each morning. You have the ability to wake up without hitting that snooze button, or take the highway to work, or spend the day in your pajamas, if you so choose. Addictions, on the other hand, become mandatory. To become an addiction, a given behavior becomes so obligatory, so compulsory, so ingrained in your ways that you're unable to avoid its performance. So you're unable to drink a cup of coffee without concurrently smoking a cigarette. You're unable to frequent a pub without drinking yourself into a stupor. You're unable to play the slot machines without exhausting all of your money. But, what makes additive behaviors mandatory? Many different influences, actually; there can be physical, emotional, and cognitive issues involved.

So, as you can see, a cigarette addiction seems much worse than a smoking habit. When addicted, you truly lose control of your behavior; cigarette smoking becomes a given, not merely an option. As such, an addiction is much more difficult to break than a habit, requiring more dedication, more perseverance, and more fortitude. Regardless of the degree of difficulty, though, addictions are conquerable. Read on.

Is your cigarette smoking habitual or addictive?

Remember, you must stop smoking cigarettes, be it habitual or addictive. The adverse health consequences mandate that you stop smoking as soon as possible. But again, you need to be prepared for the task at hand. To prepare yourself optimally, you should determine if your smoking behavior is habitual or addictive. People attempting to quit smoking may underestimate the strength of their addiction, or deny completely the presence of an addiction, and prepare themselves inadequately for the challenge. Only after they fail to quit do they acknowledge their addiction, then regarding it as insurmountable, and never again try to quit, thereby doing themselves a tremendous disservice. By preparing yourself fully for the undertaking ahead, you'll maximize your chances of success. For example, marathon runners prepare themselves for long races by running long distances during their training sessions. You can't expect to prepare for a twenty-six mile race by running only one mile per training session. Thinking such grossly underestimates the difficulty and intensity of the marathon. Marathon runners often run fifteen, twenty, or even thirty miles or more during their training sessions, because they understand how grueling a marathon can be. Similarly, you need to gauge the intensity of your preparation for your quit attempt by the extent of your addiction.

Now, there may be some smokers out there who truly are not addicted to cigarettes. Truth be known, there is a small population of smokers out there who just smoke for the heck of it, and who would have no problem throwing their cigarettes away and stopping smoking forever. However, recognize that the operative word here is "small." The fact is, most people who smoke are addicted to their cigarettes, with individuals varying only in the severity of their addictions. So, unfortunately, most of you will have a true addiction to battle. To the few truly habitual smokers out there, I offer my congratulations, and suggest that you throw out your cigarettes now and begin your lives as ex-smokers.

To the rest of you, I offer preparation for the battle with your addiction. In order to prepare yourselves, you need to discover the strength of your addiction. Before this, however, you need to simply acknowledge your addiction. Well, maybe not so simply. This is often a difficult step. We like to view ourselves as hardy, successful individuals. We don't enjoy admitting defeat, or experiencing loss. By acknowledging an addiction, you admit a weakness, a vulnerability, a defeat. By acknowledging an addiction, you state to the world that you've succumbed to a temptation. This admission isn't easy for most people. Besides, the term "addiction" itself carries such negative connotations. Addicts are those people you see on the street corner in old, ripped clothes begging for loose change. And those people sleeping on park benches. And those people on the nightly news being arrested for armed robbery. But, in order to defeat an addiction, you need to acknowledge that addiction. Recognize yourself as an addict. You can be a successful business person, a grandparent, or a valedictorian, and still be an addict. Acknowledge that you are addicted to cigarettes. Period. If you've ever stopped smoking cigarettes, then returned to smoking, you're addicted. If you've never refused a cigarette that was offered to you, you're addicted. If you've never spent a day without smoking a cigarette, you're addicted. Don't deny that you are addicted to cigarettes. Only when you admit to your addiction will you be able to move forward to combat.

Now that you recognize your addiction, we can move toward determining the strength of your addiction. There are characteristics of your smoking behavior that indicate the severity of your addiction. These have been outlined some time ago in something called the "Fagerstrom Tolerance Test." This test was originally developed by Dr. Karl Olov Fagerstrom, a Swedish researcher and a respected authority on the cigarette smoking addiction. His six-item questionnaire is widely available on the Internet, and derives a numerical score that identifies the severity of your addiction to cigarettes; the higher score you achieve, the stronger your addiction.

Let's discuss a few of these items, and understand how they reveal the intensity of your addiction. One question identifies how long it takes you to smoke your first cigarette after you awaken in the morning. The sooner you smoke that first cigarette of the day, the more points you score. Now, if you're able to wake up, shower, eat a leisurely breakfast, read the newspaper, walk the dog, drive to work, and wait until your morning coffee break before you smoke your first cigarette of the day, you're addiction is not very strong, and may be more easily defeated. However, if you sleep with a pack of cigarettes and a book of matches on your night stand so you can lean over and light up a cigarette before you even get out of bed, you have a powerful addiction which will be very difficult to overcome. Not impossible, just difficult.

Another question inquires about the number of cigarettes you smoke each day. If you only smoke a few cigarettes each day, you have a weak addiction. But if you can't let ten minutes pass without smoking a cigarette, you have a strong addiction. Understand that smoking as little as one cigarette each day can represent an addiction if you can't let a day pass without smoking that one cigarette. The more cigarettes you smoke in a day, the stronger the addiction you maintain, and the more challenging your addiction will be to conquer. Not impossible, just challenging.

I would encourage you to seek out the Fagerstrom Tolerance Test on the Internet to help you objectively assess the strength of your addiction. You might be surprised to find that you foster a large dependence on cigarettes. Don't take this information lightly. Accept the fact that you have an addiction, and develop your strategies to fight it.

Second-Hand Smoke

This is my guilt trip chapter. Unlike the remainder of this book, this chapter won't necessarily give you specific knowledge about how to stop smoking. However, I hope it will provide you with some additional motivation to quit. I'm going to tell you that your smoking habit is not just harming your health. Your habit is hurting the health of your spouse, your children, your co-workers-everyone you're close to. People you like as friends, and people you love as family, are impacted by your smoking. They can even die because of your need to smoke in their presence. Yes, this is a tremendous guilt trip; but you know what, you'll need all the motivation you need to quit smoking, so throwing in a little guilt certainly couldn't hurt. So read on, and think about the people you love as you read this section. Consider what you could be doing to their health by continuing smoking.

Anyway, so now you know about the health ills of cigarette smoking. But did you know that, by smoking, you can be imposing these very health concerns upon others? Fact is, you may be doing just that. By smoking, you may be giving heart disease, cancer, or potentially any one of these conditions to your co-workers, your spouse, or your children. The people you associate with are innocent victims of your smoking habit; in a way, you're making them smoke against their will. How are you doing this? By a vehicle called "second-hand smoke."

Now you know what "second-hand" means. This term refers to something that has already been used, and is then given to someone else to use, like an old sweater or an old toy. A hand-me-down, so to speak. "Second-hand smoke" means that you've inhaled the smoke from your cigarette, exhaled it into the air, and then allowed someone else to inhale that same smoke. Now unless you're a really mean person, I'm sure this is not your intention, and you may be shocked by my implication that you would do something so inconsiderate. The fact is, this is a completely unintentional action. Think about it. You light up your cigarette, bring it to your lips, and take in a deep breath. All this cigarette smoke is now filling every inch of your lungs, floating around, exerting its terrible influence. Some of it gets absorbed into your bloodstream to wreak havoc elsewhere in your body. Now what? You have to exhale, right? So you breathe out, and all that cigarette smoke leaves your lungs and flies out of your mouth into the air. Once there, it floats around for a real long time. You can see it; just look around yourself while you're smoking. Or look at the fog that develops in a bar, or in a smoking lounge, or anywhere else that many smokers congregate. Someone's bound to breathe in that smoke. Not that they want to, mind you; they just can't help it. People need to breathe regardless of where they're breathing. We die if we don't breathe, right. And we can only hold our breath for so long.

Try this experiment. The next time you're hanging out somewhere smoking and you know you'll be there for a while, count the number of people who walk by you while you're smoking one cigarette. Each of those people will have inhaled some of your second-hand smoke. Each of those people will have been exposed to the potential health consequences of your second-hand smoke. Now granted, we don't really know how much second-hand smoke a given individual needs to be exposed to in order to suffer ill health consequences; I'm not trying to say that everyone who walks by you will be stricken with cancer. This experiment was just to make you aware of the presence of your second-hand smoke in your environment. Besides, each non-smoker may encounter one hundred smokers in the course of his or her day; that's one hundred exposures to second-hand smoke.

Now what do we know for sure about second-hand smoke. Well, we know that chronic exposure to second-hand smoke doubles a person's chance for heart disease. Granted, the increase in risk is much larger for a smoker, but doubling your chance of something happening is still significant. Would you not play the lottery if I told you I just doubled your chance of winning? Would you bring your umbrella to work if the weatherman doubles the chance of rain? You see how even doubling the risk of heart disease is significant. And remember, since we're talking about the risk associated with chronic exposure, this would be heart disease in someone you spend a good amount of time with, smoking near, like your spouse or child. Would you want this for them?

We also know that second-hand smoke triples a person's chance of developing lung cancer. This is even more disturbing that the data on heart disease for one major reason. If you look at the causes of heart disease, cigarette smoking is certainly on the list. But so are high blood pressure, diabetes, high cholesterol, sedentary lifestyle, and obesity, among other things, all or which are fairly prevalent in society. Since there are several contributors to heart disease, one could argue that a victim of second-hand smoke may have developed heart disease anyway, because of another risk factor for such. For lung cancer, however, the list of causes is fairly short, and right on the top is cigarette smoke. Even more, the other causes of lung cancer are relatively uncommon in the general population.

Granted, someone exposed to second-hand smoke may have also worked in a shipyard forty years ago, and developed lung cancer because of exposure to asbestos. The vast majority of victims of second-hand smoke, though, will not have such a risk. Therefore, this tripling of the chance of lung cancer cannot be explained away by another factor. These people contracted lung cancer because of exposure to second-hand smoke. Your second-hand smoke. Period. Would you knowingly wish that upon someone you love? Of course not; so, now you know.

Further, we know that second-hand smoke exerts a larger effect depending on the dose received by a given individual. This means that the more a person is exposed to second-hand smoke, the greater risk he or she receives for heart disease and lung cancer. So practically speaking, the people you put at risk are those who are closest to you, those with whom you spend the most time, your friends and family, those for whom you would never wish such harm. Perfect strangers whom you encounter once in your life won't be changed much by encountering your second-hand smoke.

These are the things that we know for sure about exposure to second-hand smoke over the long term; they've been well documented in published research studies. However, we also know things subjectively about the effects of second-hand smoke in an acute setting. We know that breathing in second-hand smoke can make people dizzy and nauseous. We know that second-hand smoke can give people headaches. We know that second-hand smoke irritates the eyes and throat, and can cause a runny nose. Second-hand smoke also can further worsen breathing difficulties in people with asthma and emphysema, and can exacerbate allergic symptoms in people with seasonal allergies and sinus problems. While not life-threatening, these are bothersome symptoms that affect an individual's quality of life, and which can even put some people in the hospital. Again, not something you'd dream of imposing on a loved one.

Second-hand smoke can have an especially negative impact on the life of a child. Children are very susceptible to the effects of second-hand smoke because the defenses that make up their immune systems are weaker than those of an adult. Second-hand smoke can cause serious infections in a child, such as otitis, bronchitis, and pneumonia. Children exposed to second-hand smoke are at increased risk for having their tonsils removed because of recurrent throat infections. Also, second-hand smoke has been implicated in childhood asthma, both in causing it and in making already-existing asthma worse. In addition, exposure to second-hand smoke can stunt a child's growth. Most importantly, though, second-hand smoke has been identified as a cause of death in children; it increases the chance of sudden infant death syndrome, death from pneumonia, and death from fires in the home. In all, children who are subjected to second-hand smoke are more likely to be hospitalized, and are more likely to have frequent doctor visits for various illnesses.

In fact, second-hand smoke can negatively affect a child even before he or she is born. If a mother smokes while she's pregnant, she is at increased risk for stillbirth and miscarriage. If the child is born alive, he or she may have intellectual deficits, growth abnormalities, high blood pressure, heart and blood vessel disease, and reduced lung function. Additionally, infants born to smokers have been found to have detectable levels of carcinogens in their blood. Exposure to second-hand smoke certainly predisposes young children to lives of disability and sickness.

So now you see the potential impact that your smoking can have on the physical well-being of others. What can you do? Well, for one, quit smoking. I know, you're trying. In the meantime, don't smoke near anyone. I'm sure you're doing this already. You go outside to the porch in the cold when you want to smoke at home, or if you're visiting a friend's house. You sequester yourself into the dark recesses of your favorite restaurant-that abyss called the "Smoking Section." You miss parts of movies, needing to leave the theater to smoke. At work, you practically need to walk to another state to smoke during the day. You're probably doing all these things already. If you're not, you should, especially at home. In fact, one procedure that may actually help you quit smoking is to define your own home as a non-smoking area. Think about this. We've already outlined the health risks to you and your family that result from your smoking habit. By establishing your home as a non-smoking facility, you remove the dangers to your family while preventing yourself from smoking in the process. To extend this concept further, make a pact with yourself, out of guilt for example, that you refuse to smoke in anyone's presence. Refuse to smoke at home, at work, and in any public place in which people will be exposed to your second-hand smoke. Use your awareness of others' health help drive your quit attempt. This should encompass most of your day, and would then eliminate most of the cigarettes you smoke in a day. Doing this would benefit everyone, including yourself.

And you shouldn't just be doing these things out of consideration for others. You may need to do these things by law. For example, you're obligated not to smoke on all interstate bus trips and on any airline flight less than six hours in duration. Also, Federal law prohibits smoking at the workplace except in certain designated areas. The Occupational Safety and Health Administration and the National Institute for Occupational Safety and Health have defined cigarette smoke as a potential occupational carcinogen, and have required that workplaces create designated smoking areas with their own exhaust systems that draw second-hand smoke directly to the outside. Realize that exposure amounts in the workplace have been determined to be even greater than those in the home environment.

Do you feel guilty now? Hopefully you now realize that your habit doesn't only affect your health, but also impacts the health of those close to you. If you're going to smoke in their presence, you might as well drive drunk with them in the car. Or run across a busy highway holding their hands. Or hold their heads underwater. Use this knowledge to further motivate you to quit.

How To Begin-An Overview of the Quit Attempt

Before you begin throwing out your cigarettes, you need to understand that there is a process involved in quitting. It's a bit more involved than just tossing your cigarettes and walking away. There are stages of smoking cessation. The stage in which you find yourself will reveal your true readiness to quit, which will ultimately determine your possibility of success. We will identify these stages by name and characteristics, and attempt to place you in the appropriate stage. Furthermore, we will discuss how to advance yourself through these stages in an attempt to achieve success.

Precontemplation

Most smokers are in the first stage of smoking cessation, the precontemplation stage. The term "precontemplation" essentially means that you haven't given any thought whatsoever to stopping smoking. You enjoy smoking, you don't care about the health risks, and you don't listen to people urging you to stop smoking. You have no desire to stop smoking at all. Unfortunately, the precontemplator's chance of success is very low. Cognitive research has demonstrated that one of the strongest forces helping us to stop smoking is a true desire to stop. Sounds logical, right? If you don't want to stop smoking, why would you stop?

So how can the precontemplator be helped? If you find yourself in the precontemplation stage, don't just put this book on the shelf and let it collect dust. Even if you don't truly want to stop smoking right now, this book can still help you. Keep this book in a place where you'll see it every day. When you have some spare time, even if it's just a few minutes, pick it up and read the chapters on the ill health effects of smoking. Read it while you eat your breakfast. Read it during television commercial breaks. Read it before you go out for an evening. Read it while you're smoking. Continuously remind yourself of the negative effects of smoking on your health and well-being. Sooner or later the mere presence of the book sitting closed on your kitchen table will trigger negative thoughts about smoking. By constantly reminding yourself how bad cigarette smoking really is, you will find yourself automatically advancing to the next stage. The salient point is to be honest with yourself; analyze your own emotions about cigarette smoking as the days go by. Let the information in those chapters carry you to the next stage; you'll know when you're ready.

Contemplation

The second stage is called "contemplation." As a contemplator, you're thinking superficially about quitting, but have not yet committed yourself to the task. Several factors may be at work here. First of all, this book may finally be having an impact on your thoughts about smoking. Great! Also, you may have seen so much popular press about the negative health effects of smoking that you're becoming concerned about your own well-being. Excellent! Perhaps your friends and relatives ganging up on you week after week has grown intolerable, and you're willing to stop just to keep them quiet. Good enough! Whatever the reason, you have decided that you need to stop smoking. However, you haven't yet come up with a plan to stop. That's fine. It's very important that you want to quit smoking-remember, the desire to stop is integral to your ability to stop. Merely wanting to stop is an important first step in quitting for good.

Realize, though, that the contemplation stage is one of introspection. The external influences described above must overcome your internal desires to keep smoking before you can progress to the third stage. On the one hand are your friends, your relatives, the popular press, your doctor, and maybe even your own conscience telling you it's time to quit. On the other hand are your personal enjoyment of smoking, your brain's own dependence on your continued smoking, and the fear of the unknown. You must defeat yourself internally before you can advance further.

You can win these battles through education. Remember, you reached the contemplation stage by accepting, to some degree, that smoking is bad for you and that you need to quit. What you're lacking now is knowledge about the means to the end. You need to educate yourself by reading about smoking cessation, speaking to people who have quit smoking, attending lectures on smoking cessation-seek out everything you can about quitting. Ask questions. Search the Internet. By educating yourself on methods of smoking cessation, and especially by speaking to people who have quit smoking, you'll begin to see quitting as an attainable goal. When you view cessation as achievable, you make a tremendous stride toward quitting.

I'll give you an example. You decide that you'd love wallpaper in your living room. You go to the store, buy your supplies, pick out a pattern, and bring everything home. You stand in your living room, staring at your bare walls, surrounded by everything you bought, and come to the realization that you have no idea how to put up wallpaper. The wrong thing to do in this situation would be to put on a pair of gloves and goggles and try to hang that wallpaper. You'd likely make a mess of your living room. The right thing to do would be to read a book on hanging wallpaper, return to the store and ask an expert for tips on hanging wallpaper, and ask that friend of yours who remodeled his house last year how he hung his wallpaper. After all this self-education, you'd likely do an excellent job, and your living room would look beautiful. Through introspection, you would have recognized that you have no skill in hanging wallpaper. Through education, you would have acquired this skill. Therefore, through contemplation, you would have succeeded.

To pass through the stage of contemplation, then, you need to truly convince yourself of your commitment to quit smoking. This commitment must be real and strong. Without this degree of conviction, you'll either fail at your attempt or fall backwards into the precontemplation stage. If your commitment is strong and genuine, read on.

Preparation

After contemplation comes preparation, alternately called "ready for action." In this stage, you've accepted that smoking is bad, and you've dedicated yourself to the attempt at quitting. You've educated yourself, and you're ready to devise a plan for quitting. You're on your way. Once you reach this stage, you're chances of success are much greater, so congratulations-you're almost there. You must know, though, that the strategies you utilize in this stage, either individually or in combination, will be those that you researched and that you decided upon as an individual. You need to pick methods that are most likely to work for you, not necessarily those that worked for someone else. You will need to pick strategies that fit into your personal and work schedules, and that closely mimic your individual personality traits.

An important assignment in this stage is the identification of your individual smoking triggers. You need to identify the things in your life that make you smoke. Does stress make you smoke? Do you smoke when you meet up with certain friends? How about after lunch? By identifying the triggers of your smoking behaviors, you can prepare yourself to consciously not smoke in response to those triggers. Again, preparedness breeds success.

Write down on a piece of paper all such triggers that you can identify, leaving space between each listing for notes. You need to devise a strategy to combat each trigger before you attempt quitting. Prepare yourself for each individual challenge before you're faced with it. Again, these strategies must be individual; I can't tell you what will work for you as an individual-only you truly know that. Under each trigger that you listed, write down your solution to combating that trigger. Then leave this list someplace where you'll always see it-in your car, on the refrigerator, on your night table-so you'll never forget the plans you devised.

I'll give you a couple of examples to start you on your way. Say one of your triggers to smoking is merely waking up in the morning. You can't resist having a cigarette with your morning cup of coffee and muffin. How can you avoid smoking this cigarette? Well, for one, wake up in the morning, put on a pair of sneakers, and go for a brisk walk. By leaving your house altogether, you remove yourself physically from your cigarettes. Plus, you're getting valuable exercise time, which is important for your overall health anyway. And by the time you get home, you need to get dressed for work. You should allot your time so you don't have time for breakfast at home. That way, if you need to eat your breakfast at work, and if you work in a non-smoking facility, you've avoided your morning cigarette. You've defeated your first trigger of the day.

As another example, say you can't resist smoking cigarettes when you get together with one of your friends. You always meet up Friday nights after work, go to a local bar, share some drinks, and smoke for hours on end. How can you avoid all these cigarettes? Well, make sure you pick out some fun places to go in your neighborhood that are non-smoking facilities. When your friend calls you, recommend that you meet at one of these non-smoking places you've picked out. If he or she accepts, then by necessity he or she will be unable to smoke. If your friend doesn't smoke, then you've eliminated him or her as a trigger for your smoking behavior, and you'll avoid smoking those cigarettes, too.

One more example. You're on a long distance drive, by yourself, on a long lonely highway. Your stereo's playing your favorite CD. Your pack of cigarettes is sitting in the passenger seat right next to you, comfortably within arm's reach. There's no one to stop you from reaching for a cigarette and lighting up. How do you get yourself out of this dilemma? How do you avoid smoking those cigarettes? How to you combat those strong urges for hours on end? Pretty easily, really. Just make sure that before you embark on your drive, you remove all cigarettes from your car. If you're on that long lonely highway without cigarettes in your car, you can't smoke, right. Just don't pick up a pack when you stop for gas!

Again, take the time to list your individual triggers, come up with your own solutions to battle those triggers, and keep your list of solutions very visible. In the next stage, you will need to apply these solutions so often that they become automatic. Again, preparedness breeds success.

Another important assignment to complete during this stage is to inform the people in your life that you will be attempting to quit smoking. As I stated previously, quitting smoking is a daunting challenge; lessen the burden by sharing it with others. Tell your co-workers that you're trying to quit, so that they can watch over you while you're at work. Give them the authority to search your work space and remove any cigarettes they find. And ask them for the consideration of not smoking their cigarettes in front of you, and of not inviting you to smoke breaks anymore. Tell your family that you're trying to quit. Share your list of triggers with them, so that they may help you combat them. Keep a family member with you whenever you leave the house; you may be tempted to buy cigarettes if you go shopping alone. Enlist allies to assist you in your fight.

Your last assignment in this stage is the selection of a quit date. Walk over to your calendar with pen in hand, and mark a day in the near future on which you choose to begin your life as a non-smoker. Remember I said NEAR future. Unless it's the last week of December, you shouldn't be looking at next year's calendar. Pick a day within the next several weeks. Sometimes it helps to choose a day of significance to your life, such as your birthday or anniversary. Also, it may help to choose a day during which your other activities will be minimized; pick a day on which you don't have to work or do any strenuous chores around the house. This day should be devoted mainly to the initiation of your quit plan. Further, inform your friends and family about your quit date, further enlisting their support. Let them surround you on that day to distract you from any smoking urges you may develop.

Now all you need to do is wait. You're ready to quit smoking. You've devised plans to combat all of your triggers. You've enlisted your friends and family into the cause. You've selected your quit date. During this period of time, before your selected quit date, your mind should remain very active as you prepare yourself for the challenge. Reinforce the negative aspects of smoking through continuous self-education about the ills of smoking. Repeatedly review your smoking cessation plan with yourself, your friends, and your family. Remember, an opera singer wouldn't take the stage without thoroughly practicing his or her songs over and over again. By reviewing your plan repeatedly and daily, you will become very comfortable with your chosen strategies.

Remember, we're trying to maximize your chances of success at quitting smoking. Imagery becomes very important here. Imagine yourself as an ex-smoker. Picture yourself refusing cigarettes from passers-by. Envision yourself ridding your life of cigarettes one step at a time. Through imagery, you can defeat all of your triggers in your mind before you ever meet them in person. Envision success, and you will achieve success in the next stage.

Don't think this too far-fetched. Pitchers envision themselves throwing a strike before they pitch the ball. Orchestral soloists picture themselves playing their pieces perfectly before they play a single note. Before you implement your plan in the next stage, envision yourself as an ex-smoker, conquering your triggers one by one, throwing out your packs of cigarettes. Once you can do this with confidence, you're ready for action.

Action

Today's the day! You wake up, look at the calendar, and emblazoned across this date's box is "QUIT DATE." The day has finally come. It's your quit date. The day that you apply your affirmations, education, and convictions to your chosen goal of quitting smoking. For weeks, you've prepared yourself mentally for this day. It's time to enter the next stage, action.

To enter this stage of action, you acknowledge that you've accepted smoking as bad, committed yourself to quitting, and formulated your plan. Now, you're ready to start your non-smoking life. Only about ten percent of smokers ever enter this stage, so pat yourself on the back. You've come a very long way, and you've overcome many obstacles.

Try to conceptualize this stage as small positive steps, rather than one large jump. It may be too daunting for you to attempt to stop smoking forever in one shot; forever is a long time. Besides, unless you live forever, you may never truly feel like a success because you'll never reach forever to see if you truly quit forever. Instead, set small initial goals for yourself. Your first goal should be just to make it through your first day without smoking-some people can't even do that. If you can do that, chalk it up as success number one. After you've survived one day without cigarettes, try to last the rest of the week. Success number two. Once you've gone one whole week without smoking, try for two or three weeks. Success number three. Bolster yourself with your record of successes. With continued success comes confidence, no matter how small the goals are initially. Supported by confidence, you can proceed on to loftier goals. Go to the pub and hang out with your smoking friends. You're a success; they can't make you smoke. As you proceed onto conquering larger goals, your confidence will grow exponentially, and will drive you into the final stage of cessation.

It's important to continue your exercises in imagery into this stage. Don't just hope you'll stop smoking during this stage; make yourself stop smoking. You're not just trying to quit smoking, you have quit smoking. Live every day not as someone quitting smoking, but as an ex-smoker. From the moment you wake up on your quit date, you're an ex-smoker; you've already conquered your habit from that moment. This type of optimistic imagery, in which you picture yourself as already having achieved your goal rather than working toward your goal, will help you succeed.

The process involved in this stage is positive reinforcement. Be proud of yourself for having quit smoking once and for all. You've achieved a remarkable and important goal. Reaffirm your decision to quit by constantly reminding yourself of the negative impact of smoking, and how smart you were to quit. Brag to your friends and family, and soak up the accolades. Your happiness about your decision will further drive you to the final stage.

Maintenance

Congratulations, you're an ex-smoker. You've maintained your commitment to smoking cessation, and you haven't picked up a cigarette since your quit date. You've officially entered the maintenance stage, in which your status as an ex-smoker has become long-term.

Think of the maintenance phase as the action phase lasting forever. By now, your goals can be lofty. Whereas in the action stage, you were happy to not smoke for a day, or a week, in the maintenance stage you can conceptualize not smoking for years, and hopefully even forever, because you've succeeded at your many smaller goals of the action stage.

As you become accustomed to not smoking, you'll find it easier to refuse to smoke. By now, your trigger-blocking activities are deeply ingrained in your daily life, and have become the norm. Your friends have accepted that you no longer smoke, and have stopped offering you cigarettes; hopefully your dedication has convinced a few of them to stop smoking, too. You no longer choose to frequent restaurants and bars that you once enjoyed because of their previous association with your smoking habit. Overall, your life has changed for the better because you've stopped smoking.

How about taking your dedication one step further? Become an advocate for smoking cessation in your community. Preach to your friends about the ills of smoking, and try to convince them to quit. Join a local smoking cessation support group and describe your successes to those who are still hooked on cigarettes. Petition your old favorite restaurants to expand their non-smoking sections. Before long you'll hardly remember ever being a smoker.

However, while you may not remember, your body and brain will remind you that you once smoked, and that you enjoyed it. You will need to fight temptation along the way. This is why you need to conceptualize the maintenance stage as the action stage that lasts forever. The maintenance stage is not passive; you need to actively uphold your conviction to remain an ex-smoker every day. Again, use the power of positive reinforcement to sustain your non-smoking behavior. You've done it, you've quit smoking, you're proud of your success, and you'll never go back to smoking again.

Methods of Quitting

Alright, here we go. You're ready to quit. You've motivated yourself through the preparatory stages of the quit attempt, you've selected a quit date, and you're ready to go. Now what? Well, you need to select a method, a strategy, for quitting that you will enact on your quit date. In this chapter, we will discuss different methods you can employ for your quit attempt. These are the practical ways to quit smoking. Realize, though, that not every method will work for each smoker. You may achieve success on your first attempt, with your first choice of strategy, or you may need to try all of these strategies before you finally quit. But understand that a strategy is required. A haphazard, unplanned attempt will universally fail, guaranteed. You need to choose a plan, and enact it with confidence and diligence. For example, picture a football team running a play. What would happen if the quarterback told his players to just run around on the field and try to get open for a pass? What would happen if he brought them into the huddle and told them to run or block or tackle or do anything else they wanted to do? He'd probably get sacked by the defense on every play. That's because his teammates would have no direction, and no understanding of the goal of the play. On the other hand, if each teammate has a specific role and a specific place to run, and a specific person to block, the quarterback has a much greater chance of completing his play. And if he doesn't complete the play, he can try a different strategy to try to overcome the defense-run, pass, quarterback sneak-anything to achieve his goal of scoring a touchdown. Eventually, one plan will thwart the defense, and he'll score. The same thoughts apply to smoking cessation. Choose one strategy and give it your all. If it doesn't work, regroup and try a different strategy. Keep trying until you succeed.

Again, in this discussion it's assumed that you've progressed through the precontemplation, contemplation, and preparation stages of the quit attempt that we've discussed previously. If you haven't, you're likely not truly ready to quit and, as such, you're risk a good chance of failure should you proceed to your quit date. If you haven't worked through these stages successfully at this point, you should return to your calendar and choose a new quit date, then return to the prior chapters of this book and review. Give yourself more time to prepare emotionally and intellectually for your quit date. Remember, preparation breeds success. In order to maximize your chance for success, you need to optimize your preparedness.

Now, let's run through our smoking cessation play book.

Cold Turkey

That's right, good ol' cold turkey. Believe it or not, this method has been tested and validated in research settings. Scores of very intelligent, university-based researchers have emerged from their laboratories praising the cold turkey method of quitting smoking. Many, many people have succeeded in quitting smoking using this straight-forward technique. You can quit cold turkey. In fact, some research on smoking cessation suggests that this is the best way to quit smoking. However, you have to do it the right way. Let's go over some specifics.

First, let's talk about how not to quit cold turkey. Quitting cold turkey does not mean randomly deciding, via some immediate revelation, that you're going to stop smoking. Quitting cold turkey does not mean tossing your pack of cigarettes out of a window, in an emotional tirade, having once and for all become sick of getting short of breath every time you climb a flight of stairs. And quitting cold turkey certainly does not mean quitting on a spontaneous whim because you suddenly feel obligated to quit.

Quitting cold turkey requires much more planning than common lore would have you believe. Remember, we're talking about quitting strategies; if stopping smoking were as easy as spontaneously tossing your cigarettes into the trash one sunny morning and never puffing a cigarette again, no one would have difficulty quitting. Even quitting cold turkey requires you to plan ahead in order to achieve success.

In order to quit cold turkey, you first need to select a quit date, as we've discussed previously. After you choose your quit date, you need to keep smoking exactly as you always have. That's right, keep on smoking. Don't try to reduce the amount you smoke, and certainly don't try to stop before your quit date. The time before the arrival of your quit date should be spent preparing yourself emotionally and intellectually for the attempt. Re-educate yourself about the health ills of smoking. Imagine yourself in your mind as an ex-smoker. Use all the preparatory techniques we've reviewed previously, because on your quit date, you need to be ready to take a big jump.

In the context of quitting cold turkey, there's one important caveat that you must obey when selecting your quit date. When you decide to quit smoking cold turkey, try to make sure that no other stressors are active or expected in your life. Select a quit date that is isolated on your calendar, with no other major events, either positive or negative, planned in the near future. Granted, stressful situations are often unpredictable in their onset and impact, but avoiding them for the time being will tremendously enhance your chance of success with quitting smoking. This is very important for your ultimate success. Think about this. You're trying to stop smoking, which is stressful enough in itself. Add to this another life stress, such as tension at home, or uncertainty at work. Or even add a major positive event, such as a holiday party or other social event. What do you usually do, in normal circumstances, to relieve your everyday stresses? Chances are you smoke a cigarette. And what might you do when surrounded by your friends and colleagues at a fun party. That's right, smoke a cigarette. Therein lies the problem. By overlapping your cessation attempt with such occurrences or events, you chance exposure to one or more of your triggers for smoking behavior, and therefore would be more likely to smoke.

For example, say you decide to set your quit date for a Monday. You wake up Monday morning, throw out all you cigarettes, get dressed, and go to work. Things are great, and you couldn't be happier. You've stopped smoking, you're soaking up accolades from your peers, you're breathing more easily, and you're conquering your daily smoking triggers. Until Friday night. You forgot all about the office holiday party that was scheduled for that night. Still brimming with confidence, you put on your suit, jump into your car, and drive off to the party. After two hours of dancing, socializing, drinking and generally partying your head off, a colleague offers you a cigarette. You can't resist; too many triggers are hitting you at once, and you can't fight off them all. You succumb, and smoke a cigarette.

Another example. You decide to stop smoking two days before you meet with your boss to discuss the promotion you've been requesting. Once again, you're doing great. You haven't smoked a cigarette for the past two days. You walk into the office to meet your boss. She congratulates you on having kicked your smoking habit, but regrets to inform you that your request for a promotion was denied. Dejected, you finish out the rest of your work day, drive home, and sit on your front porch, wallowing in sorrow. After a few minutes, you get up from your chair and begin to walk down the street, trying to relieve your mind of the stress you're feeling. Denied a promotion once again. What will you tell your family? How will you afford that new car you've desired? Do you even want to work for this company anymore? But how can you start at the bottom of the corporate ladder again with a new company? Momentarily, you break through your thoughts and look up to see the corner deli. The same deli from which you've always purchased cigarettes. You find it impossible to fight your urges to smoke in light of this new stressor. You need stress relief. You walk into the deli with money in hand and buy a pack of cigarettes.

So now you see the importance of choosing a quit date that is isolated from other events in your life, be them positive or negative. You need to choose to avoid the possibility of exposure to your known triggers. Again, stress can't always be predicted, and sometimes the unpredictable will drive you to smoke again. But you must not defeat yourself. If you can foresee events or issues in the near future that may potentially thwart your quit attempt, choose a new quit date.

Now, you need to picture something for me. It's the summertime. You're at a nice resort, sitting by the pool, basking in the sun. You decide to go for a swim. You rise up from your lounge chair, fold your towel, take off your flip-flops, and stroll to the diving board. The *twenty-foot high* diving board. You climb the ladder, walk to the edge of the board, and take a deep breath. You look down at the water below, realizing that it's going to be freezing cold when you splash down. Unfettered, you clench your teeth, bend down, then leap into the air off of the board. You look down as you approach the water with ever-increasing velocity. Suddenly, you hit the water. Aaaaaahh, that's cold!!

This will be you on your quit day.

When you wake up on the morning of your quit date, take any cigarettes you have laying around the house and throw them out. Search all your coats, drawers, and shirt pockets. Go out to your car and remove all the cigarettes you find. When you get to work, empty out the drawers of your desk, or the pockets of your uniform; remove all cigarettes from your work space. Remove all cigarettes from your life. Period. This, officially, is quitting cold turkey. This is jumping off the diving board and going for it. Sure it's sudden, but it's assumed that you've progressed through the proper stages of the quit attempt and prepared yourself emotionally and intellectually for this moment. You're ready for the plunge.

After you rid your house, your work environment, your car, and your life of cigarettes, carry on with your day. Have breakfast, get to work, take a morning jog-do whatever you would have done on any other day. Remember, this should be the only major change in your life currently. Your daily life should proceed as usual, with the exception of you being an ex-smoker.

Say it with me now-an *ex*-smoker.

As this first day of quitting cold turkey proceeds, the first challenge you will encounter will be your triggers. But remember, you're prepared to face them. You've developed strategies to combat your triggers, and you've posted them on your refrigerator. You've reviewed them every day since you selected your quit date. Now is the time to put your plans into action. You wake up in the morning longing for a cigarette-put on your sneakers and go for a jog. You arrive at work, knowing you'll have to walk past the usual crowd of smokers congregated at the front door, having a last smoke before the work day begins-walk around the building and enter through the back door. It's lunch time, and your colleagues are inviting you to the pub down the street for hamburgers and cigarettes-tell them you brought your lunch from home, and will be eating at the office. Use your strategies to beat your triggers. Don't worry, they will work. And remember, with each success comes confidence. You can defeat your triggers, and you can stop smoking.

The second challenge you will face is the experience of nicotine withdrawal. This may have already started, from the moment you woke up. Or it may start a few hours after you wake up. But it's going to happen. But again, you've expected it and prepared for it. If deemed necessary, you've employed your nicotine replacement method of choice. You've determined your modes of distraction for when strong urges arise. Remember that these symptoms should only last a few days, so hang on and beat them.

That's it, essentially. That's quitting cold turkey. It's a little more involved than common lore suggests, but still relatively straight-forward. If you're willing to take a big jump, you may achieve success. Just make sure to continually present yourself as an ex-smoker from the morning of your quit date. Just as we discussed the importance of imagery previously, the importance of a positive self-presentation is immeasurable. Whereas before you imagined yourself as an ex-smoker, now you are an ex-smoker. Think as such, and you will act as such. Act as such, and you'll leave cigarettes behind you forever.

Rapid Smoking

To present the completely opposite approach to smoking cessation, I give you "rapid smoking." Rapid smoking is a less-often used technique because of its sheer brutality. Whereas I likened quitting cold turkey to jumping into a pool of cold water from a high diving board, quitting with rapid smoking is akin to crushing a beer can on your head. It's brutal and violent, but it may just get the job done.

The nice thing about quitting by rapid smoking, as you will see, is the relative lack or preparation you'll need prior to your quit attempt. You don't even neces-sarily need to select a quit date; you can wake up one morning and decide to try rapid smoking, and it might still work. Also, if you try rapid smoking one day and find yourself unsuccessful, you can just try it again the next day. And if you fail again, try again. You can even perform rapid smoking several times in one day. As a matter of fact, if you have the courage to do rapid smoking multiple times in one day, you'll likely be even more likely to quit smoking. This element of spontaneity is the major benefit of this method of quitting.

Another benefit of this method is that it propagates a true aversion to cigarettes. If you speak to ex-smokers who haven't smoked a cigarette for several years, they may tell you that they can't stand the smell of cigarette smoke anymore. These people have developed a true aversion to cigarette smoke, whereby the mere smell of cigarettes burning makes them feel physically ill, almost nauseous. With rapid smoking, you hope to develop this degree of distaste for cigarettes in a matter of minutes. Sounds magical? Read on.

To prepare yourself for rapid smoking, simply choose a location for your attempt. Try not to choose a public space. Definitely don't try this at home, especially if you have a spouse and children. A space outdoors would be preferable. Otherwise, select a location in which you know you'll be alone for quite some time. Realize that after your rapid smoking attempt, you'll leave behind a lot of second-hand smoke.

Are you curious, yet? Then let's start our rapid smoking attempt. Walk around your house, collect all the books of matches and packs of cigarettes you can find, and put them into a bag. Go to your car and add any cigarettes and matches you find to your bag. Then, with bag in hand, proceed to the location chosen for your attempt.

When you arrive at your chosen location, prepare yourself for war; the battle that lies ahead will be fierce and swift. Open the bag, take out a cigarette, light up, and start smoking. But don't just smoke like you're relaxing after a nice cup of flavored coffee. Remember, this is *rapid* smoking. You need to smoke that cigarette down to the end as quickly as you can. Puff on that cigarette with every breath. You should certainly stop for a bit if you become very short of breath, dizzy, or lightheaded, and you should also stop if you experience any chest discomfort. Otherwise, keep on puffing as quickly as you can. When you finish that cigarette, light up another and keep smoking as rapidly as you can. Keep smoking until you truly can't bear the thought of lighting up one more cigarette and taking even one more puff. At this point, pick up your bag with the remaining cigarettes and throw them out. That's it; that's rapid smoking.

Are you winded? Nauseous? Weak? Sick? Good. Do you feel like smoking a cigarette now? I'm sure you don't. Hopefully you've developed the true aversion to cigarettes that we're hoping for. If this worked, you'll feel this same way whenever you see someone smoking, whenever you smell cigarette smoke, whenever you see an advertisement for cigarettes in a magazine, and whenever someone offers you a cigarette. What you've done is reprogrammed your brain to recognize cigarettes as toxic, harmful, and distasteful. Remember that your brain sees cigarettes as good because of the activation of reward and pleasure pathways, which become a challenge to your cessation. Well, you're brain should definitely change its mind about smoking after this onslaught. By rapid smoking, you're beating your brain into submitting to your desire not to smoke by redefining cigarette smoking as aversive rather than pleasurable. Now, the thought of cigarette smoke will activate memories of nausea and sickness, which will then reinforce your cessation.

Now I probably wouldn't try this method if you have high blood pressure, heart disease or emphysema, or if you've had strokes in the past. Your heart and lungs probably won't tolerate well the pummeling to which you would subject them by rapid smoking. But if you're free of such conditions, this method is worth a try. It's wicked, it's intense, and it just might work.

Nicotine and Cigarette Tapering

Falling between these two extremes are the methods of nicotine and cigarette tapering. Tapering has been most touted in the context of nicotine replacement aids, but you can control your own taper with cigarettes, too. In fact, tapering with cigarettes may afford you less of an adjustment compared to tapering with some other aid. Not that nicotine replacement aids are without merit, but you may find it easier to stop smoking by tapering cigarettes, which you're already used to, rather than by abruptly replacing your cigarettes with, say, patches or gum. For example, you may find an acoustic guitar song difficult to play if you've practiced the song on an electric guitar. And you may find it difficult to play a song on a violin if you've practiced that song on a cello. By using that with which you are familiar, the change is less drastic and thereby easier to handle.

Let's define the terms first, then discuss how we can employ these methods of quitting. The application of both of these methods will be on your quit date. Nicotine tapering means that, upon your quit date, you continue to smoke as many cigarettes as before, but you choose cigarettes of lower nicotine content. So if you currently smoke regular cigarettes, you'll start smoking lighter cigarettes. If you smoke unfiltered cigarettes, start choosing cigarettes with a filter. The benefit of nicotine tapering lies in the fact that as your day progresses, you're smoking the same number of cigarettes as usual, including all of your favorites. Smoke with breakfast, smoke after dinner, smoke with your friends. Every time you have an urge to smoke, grab a cigarette and smoke. The kicker is that these cigarettes have less nicotine, so in the process of seemingly smoking as usual, you're actually reducing your total daily intake of addictive nicotine by a substantial amount. In this way, by choosing several different cigarette brands of decreasing nicotine content, sooner or later you'll be inhaling a very little amount of nicotine compared to that which you're body is accustomed. Your body and brain can grow used to functioning without nicotine gradually, so that when you finally stop smoking altogether, your withdrawal symptoms will be minimized. You'll actually suppress, and hopefully prevent, the development of uncomfortable withdrawal symptoms which would otherwise tempt you to start smoking again.

Cigarette tapering involves consciously smoking fewer cigarettes, in a stepwise fashion, over the course of a day. For example, if you normally smoke forty cigarettes daily, reduce that number to thirty on your quit date. One week later, reduce that number to twenty. One week after that, reduce it to ten. Hopefully after that step, you'll be able to stop smoking altogether. The theory here, again, is that you're reducing your total daily intake of nicotine slowly. The difference is that you smoke your usual cigarettes, but fewer of them in a day. In this fashion, you gradually reduce your daily nicotine intake, and hopefully curb the development of withdrawal symptoms and cravings.

You can choose one or the other of these methods, or you can combine them into a nicotine/cigarette tapering plan. Whichever you choose, though, you need to be able to calculate your daily intake of nicotine in order to devise your ultimate plan. In order to figure this out, look on you cigarette package for the nicotine content of your cigarettes. Multiply this number by the number of cigarettes you smoke each day. This result is your current total daily nicotine intake. Now, with each step you define, repeat this calculation to determine the decrement in your total daily nicotine intake.

Now, there are several problems you need to be aware of when using these techniques, and they all center around one important element-you create the plan. You would think that this would be wonderful, in that you're in control of your own quit attempt. You want to stop, and you're in control; this should work just fine, right? However, without diligence and dedication, and without a realistic plan, these methods can easily lead to failure. Remember, no matter how much control you seem to have over these techniques, you still need to actively combat your urges, your triggers, and your brain. You cannot be simply a passive participant in these strategies; you must remain cognizant of your goal of smoking cessation, and must be aware of situations in which you could potentially veer from that plan.

Let's begin to illustrate some potential failures with the nicotine tapering method first. You decide to step down from forty high nicotine cigarettes to forty low nicotine cigarettes on your quit date. You smoke every cigarette as usual, and succumb to every urge, with the assurance that your cigarettes have less nicotine. You've done your math, and you've reduced your daily nicotine intake substantially. You feel great, and you're quitting smoking. Everything's fine, until you go to the deli to purchase another carton of low nicotine cigarettes and open up an empty wallet. A quick mental tally helps you come to the discovery that over the past few weeks you've bought twice the number of cartons of cigarettes as before. You've been smoking eighty cigarettes each day! How did this happen? Well, since you're inhaling less nicotine per cigarette, you'll likely experience more urges as the day passes. The mistake often made in the context of nicotine tapering is to smoke more cigarettes for each urge, smoking two or three instead of just one in order to quell withdrawal symptoms. The key is to consciously smoke as many cigarettes as before and no more. Don't allow your brain to lure you to compensate for the lower nicotine intake by forcing you to smoke more cigarettes.

I'll give you another example with cigarette tapering. You decide to speak to one of your friends who is trying to quit smoking by cigarette tapering. You remember the day ten months ago when he told you he was starting his taper; at the time, he was smoking sixty cigarettes each day. You call him on the phone to see if he was able to quit. He tells you that cigarette tapering is the best; he hasn't experienced a single withdrawal symptom in ten months. You ask him if he's stopped smoking yet. He tells you that he hasn't, but he's down to fifty-five cigarettes a day. Isn't that great? No, it's not, actually. At this rate, it would take him ten years to stop smoking. Why even bother trying to quit? The lesson learned is that with cigarette tapering, you need to set a realistic time goal to make the attempt meaningful. Otherwise, you might as well keep smoking. Expect to taper to zero over one to two months at the most.

In summary, the degree of control over your quit attempt that cigarette and nicotine tapering afford can work to your detriment without the employment of a reasonable amount of will power. Granted, these methods still may be more tolerable than trying to quit cold turkey, but you still need to realize that urges and withdrawal symptoms will occur. You need to be cognizant of when and why you drift away from your plan. Whichever technique you choose, devise your plan and time course before your quit date. Calculate the reduction of daily nicotine intake that occurs with each step. Mark the dates of your steps, as well as your quit date, on your calendar, and adhere to them strictly without compromise.

Quit Contract

Yet another method of quitting smoking is through the creation of a quit contract. A quit contract is not necessarily a technique for smoking cessation; it's more of a plan, or an agreement to quit smoking. The appealing element of the quit contract is the fact that you involve others in your smoking cessation plan. We know that, for the most part, goals are best achieved by a team rather than by an individual. For example, try to move a sofa across your living room by yourself. Difficult, right? Now call over three of your friends to help. The sofa is now much easier to move. Likewise, you may achieve your goal of smoking cessation if you form a team to help you.

To create a quit contract, list the names of all your friends and family members who smoke cigarettes. Call them individually to determine their willingness to try to quit smoking. Hopefully, some of them will be interested in quitting, too. Collect the names of those who are interested on a separate list, then coordinate a meeting with them to discuss the quit contract. You will create a pact amongst all in the group to stop smoking together. All those in favor of this plan should agree to reconvene on a universally chosen quit date, and then periodically thereafter. Also, everyone agreeing to quit smoking should exchange phone numbers and other contact information, such as e-mail addresses.

In theory, the quit contract has several advantages. For one, you're making peer pressure work for you, not against you. Usually, peer pressure causes you to smoke because everyone else in your group is smoking, and not smoking would make you feel isolated and alone. In the creation of a quit contract, you reverse peer pressure by inventing the rules of the group. In fact, you control peer pressure altogether. Remember, this is your group; you're the leader of the pack. For example, you decree that anyone wanting to be a member of your group has to wear a blue T-shirt. If someone wants to be in your group, they'd better buy a pack of blue T-shirts. They'd feel detached if they showed up for a group meeting in a red T-shirt when everyone else was wearing a blue T-shirt. So, as leader of this group, as the head honcho, you decide that people can't be in your group if they smoke. Only ex-smokers can be members of your group. So now, peer pressure will actually encourage those in the group to stop smoking, driving everyone toward cessation. Since everyone will be quitting smoking, you'll feel isolated and alone if you start smoking again, and you'll be more likely to decide not to smoke if the temptation arises.

Another advantage of the quit contract is in the establishment of your own support group. By deciding to share the smoking cessation experience with others, you establish your own network of people who fully understand the challenge you face simply because they're experiencing the same challenge at the same time. They recognize how strong an urge can feel. They understand the abundance of triggers that can entice you to return to smoking. Overall, they know how difficult stopping smoking can be, and they can be called upon to offer you sympathy, guidance, advice, and encouragement when needed. For example, say you find yourself alone on a long drive. You suddenly experience a strong urge for a cigarette. Conveniently, a roadside service center is only two miles ahead. You fight the urge to pull into the service center to buy a pack of cigarettes, but you feel that it's becoming overwhelming. Concerned, you call one of your group members for advice. She tells you that whenever she's driving and feels a strong craving, she distracts herself by looking at the license plates of nearby cars for a certain letter or number. Intrigued, you hang up the phone and start looking for the letter "H" in every license plate you see. Before long, your craving has dissipated and the service center is seven miles behind you. Her advice helped prevent you from relapsing into smoking again, whereas you may have started smoking again if left to your own impulses.

A third benefit of the quit contract borders on paranoia, but is effective just the same. Every member of your group represents a pair of eyes to watch your every move. A good group member will watch you for suspicious activity that might seem suggestive of a potential return to smoking behavior, and will stop you in your tracks. In this light, it's smart to include in your group an assortment of family members, friends, and co-workers; in this way, some member of your group will be with you throughout your day to stop you should you try to smoke. So when you try to sneak out to the backyard after breakfast for a quick smoke, your spouse can block you. And when you try to creep out the back door of the office for a cigarette, your co-worker can follow you out and stop you. And when you steal away to the corner of the bar for a cigarette, your friends can gang up on you. It's very helpful to have others around to keep you in check at times when you find it difficult to keep yourself in check.

Yet another benefit of the quit contract lies in the spirit of competition. People are more likely to rise to a given task when instituted as a contest. For instance, you may bowl a score of 104 when just playing for fun, but might bowl a score of 146 if your friend wagers ten dollars on the game. Your mind set becomes more intense; you're not going to lose those ten dollars! To use this in the context of a quit contract, set up a punishment system within your group, such that anyone who smokes suffers some penalty. I'm not talking about cruel things, but rather benign consequences for relapsing to smoking behavior. For example, make a rule that anyone who smokes must treat the entire group to dinner on a Thursday night. Or anyone who smokes must treat the entire group to a round of drinks at the bar. Now, smoking cessation becomes competitive. You're not going to be the one to treat the entire group. You're going to win, and let someone else treat. Luckily, by winning this contest, you'll also be quitting smoking.

Summary

These are the different methods of smoking cessation. One of them should work for you. If not, try another one. Or repeat one you tried before. Most importantly, keep trying. Eventually, one of these methods should help you achieve success. Remember, quarterbacks rarely score a touchdown on their first play. They run, they pass, they hand-off; they try several different strategies to achieve success. And if they can't score on their own, they get help from their teammates. Keep trying, and you'll score, too.

Medications and Nicotine Replacement Methods

In this chapter, we'll discuss the traditional assistive agents used in smoking cessation, nicotine replacement therapies and medication. These are available either over-the-counter or by prescription. While they are not essential for quitting smoking, we'll discuss why some people find it easier to quit with them.

Nicotine Replacement Therapy

There are many different types of nicotine replacement agents. There are patches, gums, sprays, and inhalers. Some are used once daily, and some need to be used several times each day. Deciding which one to use may seem daunting, but there is a simple answer to this issue. Use whichever you want. You may feel comfortable with putting on a patch in the morning and forgetting about it for the rest of the day. Or, you may prefer inhalers because you'll still feel like you're smoking cigarettes. Or perhaps you like chewing gum in general, so a nicotine gum would be ideal for you. Choose the agent with which you would feel most comfortable.

Regardless of the form of nicotine replacement you choose, their basic utility lies in the substitution of nicotine in another form for the nicotine in cigarettes. As we've discussed in a previous chapter, while you have an addiction to cigarettes, the actual addictive agent is nicotine. You smoke cigarettes because of your addiction to nicotine, cigarettes being the only practical way for you to get nicotine into your system. So your nicotine addiction supports your smoking habit. Enter the nicotine replacement therapies, which deliver nicotine to your system in another way. By using nicotine replacement therapies, then, you can separate your addiction to nicotine from your habit of cigarette smoking. With your addiction managed, you can concentrate your conscious efforts on kicking your habit of cigarette smoking. Research has demonstrated the benefit of nicotine replacement in helping people quit smoking.

The major noticeable benefit of nicotine replacement therapy is the elimination of withdrawal symptoms. Remember, these symptoms often drive people back to smoking simply through their annoyance, persistence, and severity. By using nicotine replacement, you can eliminate the cravings you might otherwise experience when you stop smoking. In this way, you can fully address any other surrounding issues fostering your smoking habit. As you've seen in this book, quitting smoking is an emotionally and mentally laborious process, requiring introspection and concentration. You don't need nicotine withdrawal symptoms distracting your attention away from this process. How well would you be able to concentrate on an exam if someone stood right next to you, tapping your shoulder as you took the test? By using nicotine replacement therapies, you can remove the distraction of nicotine withdrawal symptoms, freeing your mind to focus on your techniques of smoking cessation.

A second noticeable benefit lies in your achievement of control over your addiction. As a smoker, you lack control; hence, the concept of being addicted. You are unable to stop yourself from smoking cigarette after cigarette, again because of your addiction to nicotine. Your brain causes you to experience intense cravings when you don't smoke, cravings that are only satisfied by nicotine. Typically, you would supply your brain with this nicotine by smoking a cigarette; thereby, again, your addiction drives your habit. But your brain doesn't necessarily care how it gets that nicotine. By providing that nicotine to your brain by another means, your brain will leave you alone, so to speak. By using nicotine replacement, then, you'll find it much easier to refuse a cigarette, because your brain won't be pestering you to smoke for nicotine. You'll have the nicotine replacement agent supplying nicotine to your brain, so what purpose would the cigarette serve? Through the ability to refuse to smoke a cigarette, you gain a degree of control over your habit; and being able to refuse cigarettes is a tremendous booster of your confidence in your ability to quit for good.

The third provision of nicotine replacement therapy is that of an active first step in your cessation attempt. Quitting smoking is a life-changing event, with huge implications. You'll be stopping something you've done for perhaps thirty or forty years, every day, several times each day. You'll be removing something that is a large part of your being, your personality, your image. You'll be redefining yourself as an ex-smoker. This is a big event, surrounded by plenty of personal drama and fraught with internal conflict; it would be nice to have something to show the world that proves your commitment. Purchasing a nicotine replacement agent can represent a defining first step for your attempt. It marks your commitment to the attempt, your decision to quit. It's concrete, not nebulous. It's tangible, not cerebral. You can hold it in your hand, put it on your kitchen counter, and show it off to your friends. It's a practical, external representation of your internal desire to quit smoking. Think about it this way. What do some people do before starting a new job? They buy new suits. The suits are their external representation of their internal readiness for their new positions; they buy new suits to reveal their confidence in themselves, that they expect to shine both externally with their clothes and internally through their words. Likewise, by purchasing a nicotine replacement agent, you acquire palpable evidence of your commitment to quit that you can hold in your own hands. It helps you show the world that you are truly ready to quit for good.

As good as nicotine replacement therapy sounds, it is not without its problems. For one, you need to be wary of developing an addiction to your chosen nicotine replacement agent. Remember, nicotine replacement agents still contain nicotine, which is addictive no matter how you take it in. Sure, you may not be smoking cigarettes anymore, but you may be chewing forty pieces of nicotine gum daily, or putting on five nicotine patches at once. To phrase this another way, you may have stopped smoking, which is great because you avoid exposure to an innumerable amount of carcinogens; but, you're still addicted to nicotine, which could ultimately trigger a return to smoking behavior if not recognized and checked. This is a very important concept for you to recognize. Always remember that there are two issues you need to tackle in smoking cessation-the habit of smoking, and the addiction to nicotine. Ultimately, your addiction to nicotine fuels your habit of cigarette smoking. You may be able to kick the habit, but don't discount the importance of the addiction. For example, imagine you're addicted to alcohol. You drink about twenty cans of beer every day, and you want to stop. So, you cut down your beer ingestion and squelch your withdrawal symptoms with vodka. Before long, you're not drinking beer anymore, but you're going through two bottles of vodka every day. It's great that you're no longer drinking beer, but you're still addicted to alcohol; you've just substituted one form for another. The same principle applies to smoking cessation agents. If you're not careful, you may just replace your addiction to cigarettes with a new addiction to a nicotine replacement agent. And if you maintain this addiction to nicotine, it's an easy next step to buy a pack of cigarettes and start smoking again; cigarettes are more readily available in the community than nicotine replacement agents, anyway.

In order to avoid this, set a schedule for yourself whereby you gradually taper the use of your chosen nicotine replacement agent over time. Remember that your use of these agents gives you control over your habit and your addiction. To use them properly, just control how much you use. As an illustration, let's use nicotine gum. To taper your use of gum, chew twenty pieces of gum daily for the first week, fifteen for the second, ten for the third, and five for the fourth, then stop use of the gum. Try not to take extra pieces unless absolutely necessary for uncontrollable withdrawal symptoms. An easy way to accomplish this would be to carry with you only that number of pieces scheduled for that day, plus one for an emergency. So if you're starting your taper with twenty pieces of gum, put twenty-one pieces in your pocket, or handbag, or briefcase at the start of the day, and leave the rest of your supply of gum at home. If you only carry twenty-one pieces with you, there's no way you can take anymore that day, so you've effectively limited your nicotine intake for the day.

Another important way to avoid becoming addicted to your nicotine replacement agent is to remember that your taper should be performed gradually. Don't expect to taper yourself over three or four days. If you try to taper use to quickly, you'll experience frequent withdrawal symptoms, which would trigger frequent emergency use of your nicotine replacement agent. In using these agents, you're trying to eliminate the experience of withdrawal symptoms; you'll do this most effectively by taking your time. Make sure your dose reductions come no more frequently than once weekly.

A second problem with nicotine replacement agents is logical, but often unrecognized. Nicotine replacement therapy will not make you quit. Remember, nicotine replacement therapy functions to eliminate withdrawal symptoms while you deal with the behavioral and emotional issues that drive your smoking habit. As a smoker trying to quit, you still need to actively deal with those issues. Nicotine replacement agents are often likened to some form of auto-pilot; whereby an individual will slap on a patch, or chew a piece of gum, and expect to suddenly and magically stop smoking without any concentrated effort on his or her part.

This is a very common mistake with respect to the use of smoking cessation aids in general, and there are some reasons why this perception is so prevalent. First of all, as we have stated previously, stopping smoking is emotionally challenging. In order to quit successfully and truly, you need to employ powerful introspection to discover the underlying issues driving your smoking behavior, and then work actively to develop and apply methods to combat these drives. Along the way, you battle temptations and triggers constantly. Some people just don't want to bother with all of this, and look for an easier way to quit smoking. In this quest for the easy way out, so to speak, they turn to nicotine replacement therapy as a way of avoiding this introspective process, hoping that their chosen agent will make them quit. They adopt a passive role in their own quit attempt, expecting their nicotine replacement agents to actively cause them to quit while they sit back as spectators to the process. This is called using nicotine replacement therapy as a crutch. Think about how crutches work. Crutches help you to walk if you sprain an ankle, or break a leg, or otherwise hurt yourself such that you find it difficult to walk. But, you would still need to walk. You can't just hold onto crutches and have them swoop you around to wherever you need to go. You still need to actively put one foot in front of the other and walk, using the crutches as assistive devices in your goal to ultimately walk again without them. However, sometimes, people find it easier to walk with the crutches than to suffer through training to walk without them; so, they become reliant on their crutches, improperly using them all the time and neglecting their rehabilitation. Always remember that nicotine replacement agents, like crutches, are merely assistive devices. While they will not carry you to your goal, they can help you to achieve your goal more easily if you work at it actively.

In addition, nicotine replacement therapy advertising can mislead people into thinking that these agents can replace your active methods of quitting smoking. The next time you're watching television, pay particular attention to the commercials for nicotine replacement agents. See if they mention the proven efficacy of these agents; chances are, they will. See if they mention how easy they are to use; chances are, they will. Then, see if they mention that these agents have never been shown to work in the absence of concurrent cognitive and behavioral therapy; chances are, they won't. Reviewing the published studies on the benefits of nicotine replacement therapy reveals that they are tested in the context of cognitive and behavioral therapy sessions, during which participants discuss the personal issues that govern their smoking habit. Notice that commercials for nicotine inhalers never show smokers in group therapy sessions, puffing on their inhalers. Commercials for nicotine gum never show a smoker chewing gum while meeting with an addiction counselor. Instead, commercials glamorize nicotine replacement agents by depicting people jumping into convertibles, going on dates, or hanging out with friends without a care in the world as their nicotine addiction is eliminated while they're having the time of their lives. This is understandable, of course. The makers of these products need to sell their products, so they make their use appear fun, appealing, and effortless. You, as the consumer, need to place these agents into their appropriate context. While commercials may lead you to believe that stopping smoking is as easy as slapping on a patch, or puffing on an inhaler, you know better. Now you don't have to enroll yourself in a formal program to use these agents; however, just keep in mind that quitting smoking is never without individual effort.

As a final caution toward the use of nicotine replacement therapy, be careful if you have medical conditions that put you at risk for heart attacks or strokes, because their use in these contexts may be dangerous. If you have high blood pressure or blood vessel disease, you may be wise to avoid nicotine replacement therapy altogether. Also, there are medical concerns for those who continue to smoke while using nicotine replacement agents. Yes, some people will continue to smoke while they simultaneously use nicotine replacement therapy. This is very dangerous, as it can easily lead to nicotine overdose. Besides, if you find yourself doing this, you need to recognize that you're obviously not ready to quit smoking.

Zyban

The world was introduced to Zyban very recently, but the actual medication, bupropion, has been on the market much longer. Zyban was originally introduced to the world as Wellbutrin, an antidepressant. After practitioners noticed that their depressed patients stopped smoking, formal studies were ordered on Wellbutrin in the context of smoking cessation. From the favorable results of these studies, Zyban was born.

Bupropion, the parent compound for both Wellbutrin and Zyban, is available in both rapid-release and sustained-release forms, the latter being used for smoking cessation. Bupropion works in the brain to combat the reward system that supports your smoking habit; we have discussed this system already. This reward system acts to promote smoking behavior by identifying smoking as pleasurable, and stopping smoking as unpleasant. Bupropion interrupts this reward system, so that your brain can no longer signal to you that smoking is pleasurable.

Used for smoking cessation, Zyban is prescribed twice daily for at least seven weeks, with some researchers touting as much as fifty-two weeks of therapy. These recommendations are based on studies that confirmed the efficacy of Zyban compared to a placebo pill (a fake pill with no active component); twice as many people taking Zyban quit smoking compared to those who did not. Furthermore, the effectiveness of Zyban increases when combined with a nicotine patch.

The common side effects of Zyban include dry mouth, muscle and joint aches, dizziness, tremors, palpitations, nausea, constipation, and mouth ulcers. More seriously, Zyban can cause seizures, especially in patients with a history of seizure or tumors of the brain. Further, it is generally recommended that Zyban not be used by pregnant women, although no proof of actual harm exists.

Clonidine

Clonidine is used traditionally in the treatment of high blood pressure. It works in the brain, and its presence causes the blood vessels to relax, thereby lowering the blood pressure. It is available as a rapidly-acting pill, which must be taken several times each day, or as a long-acting patch, which delivers medication through the skin. Some side effects of clonidine include dizziness, dry mouth, constipation, anorexia, excessive nighttime, depression, and palpitations. Clonidine can have adverse reactions with other blood pressure medications and with antidepressants.

As far as smoking cessation is concerned, clonidine theoretically works by reducing the experience of nicotine withdrawal symptoms, again through its influence on the brain and nervous system. The fact is that clonidine does work. People who use clonidine during their smoking cessation attempts are almost twice as likely to stop smoking as those who don't use it, all other things being equal. This finding has been confirmed and validated. Clonidine is also very convenient, being available in a once-weekly patch.

The issue with the use of clonidine for smoking cessation is that of risk versus benefit. For every action we take, there is a risk and a benefit. Whenever we make a decision to act, we determine if the benefits of that action would outweigh the potential risks of that action. If the benefits outweigh the risk, we act; however, if the risks outweigh the benefits, we halt. For example, let's talk about driving down the street towards an intersection, at which the traffic light just turned yellow. You could step on the gas and speed past the changing light; the benefit would be not having to wait several minutes at a red light. The risk, however, would be getting into an accident if the light turns red and oncoming traffic begins to move. You need to decide if beating the light would be worth the risk of getting into a car accident before you step on the gas. And so, you would need to decide if the benefit of quitting smoking would be worth the risk of experiencing the side effects of clonidine.

Mecamylamine

Mecamylamine is also a medication that is typically used for high blood pressure. It is categorized as a ganglionic blocking agent, which means that it tempers impulses that travel along nerves that ultimately contribute to high blood pressure. It is available as a rapidly-acting pill. Some side effects of mecamylamine include fatigue, tremors, sedation, constipation, dry mouth, swelling of the tongue, dizziness, and retention of urine. Mecamylamine is not recommended for people with glaucoma or heart disease.

For smoking cessation, mecamylamine functions as an antagonist of nicotine; like bupropion, it blocks the reward system that nicotine establishes in the brain, which we have discussed previously. It does seem that mecamylamine has some efficacy for smoking cessation, but not by itself. When used alone, mecamylamine has not demonstrated efficacy for cessation. However, it has been shown to increase the effectiveness of nicotine replacement therapies and Zyban. For example, people using mecamylamine with a nicotine patch quit more often than those using just mecamylamine, or just a patch. This finding is not unusual in medicine, or in life for that matter. By combining mecamylamine with another agent, you attack your smoking habit, and your nicotine addiction, from two different directions, and at two different points, thereby increasing the effectiveness of your attack. Think about it this way. Say you need to clean your kitchen. On the one hand, you could take on the entire task yourself, but that would take lots of time and effort. On the other hand, you could enlist someone to help you. Now, while you clean the sink, someone else wipes down the table. While you dust the cabinets, someone else mops the floor. You achieve your goal of a clean kitchen more easily and more quickly. This same principle applies to the increased success realized from combining these methods of smoking cessation. The combination of mecamylamine with nicotine replacement therapy or Zyban works better than either method alone.

Again, the matter of risk versus benefit applies. By using two agents instead of one, you increase your chance of quitting; however, you also increase your chance of experiencing side effects from either or both agents. You would, again, need to decide if the increase in efficacy is worth the risk of side effects.

Nortriptyline

Nortriptyline is a tricyclic antidepressant medication, so named for its triple ring biochemical structure, which is used traditionally for the treatment of major depression. We don't know exactly how nortriptyline works for depression, but it is known that it blocks several chemical pathways in the brain. Its mechanism in smoking cessation seems similar to that of Zyban, blocking the reward pathways that promote the smoking habit. Important side effects of nortriptyline include high blood pressure, heart rhythm disturbances, retention of urine, confusion, panic, anxiety, and abdominal cramping. Nortriptyline may impair the ability to drive a car or operate heavy machinery. There is also a withdrawal associated with this medication, with symptoms including headache, nausea, and weakness. People with heart disease and hyperthyroidism would be wise to avoid this medication, because of the possible development of fatal heart rhythm disturbances. Finally, the safety of nortriptyline for pregnant women has not been established.

But does nortriptyline work for smoking cessation. Yes, actually. When studied, nortriptyline was effective in helping people quit smoking; over twice as many people taking the medication were able to stop smoking compared to those not taking it. Nortriptyline worked especially well for highly addicted smokers. Further, although success waned over the subsequent six months, more users of nortriptyline remained free of cigarettes compared to those who didn't take it. So nortriptyline does work but, as above, you need to weigh the possibility of serious side effects when considering this medication.

Silver Acetate

Silver acetate is a hazardous chemical compound that is harmful if swallowed, and which has been classified as a moderate health risk, causing headache, eye irritation, dizziness, and difficulty breathing. Silver acetate for smoking cessation is marketed as a spray, lozenge, or gum. It's effectiveness in this context lies in the unpleasant taste produced when combined with cigarette smoke; if a smoker encounters an unpleasant taste while smoking, he or she would be less likely to smoke. Unfortunately, silver acetate has not been demonstrated as effective for smoking cessation. This is all I'm saying about this, because based on the clearly defined health risks, you would be silly to even consider using it.

Summary

Now that we have discussed the various medications and nicotine replacement therapies used for smoking cessation, the question remains as to which, if any, you should use. A few important points need to be mentioned and reinforced here. First, you need to understand the difference between a study population and a regular population. Research studies, for the most part, employ groups of patients in a study population. These study populations differ greatly from the regular population around us. Let's discuss the Zyban research as an example. The people involved in the Zyban studies were enrolled in formal behavioral and cognitive therapy programs, including both individual and group sessions, during the time they were taking the medication. They were also followed over the long term via telephone contact with those conducting the studies after they stopped taking the medication. So they were watched very closely, and had several different people to whom to answer about their smoking behavior. Also, their underlying issues driving their smoking behaviors were explored in therapy sessions. Then, once they stopped smoking, their abstinence was reinforced by telephone contact for up to one year thereafter. In contrast, the typical users of Zyban in the regular population pick up a prescription from their physicians, who provide an average of five minutes of counseling on smoking cessation. After that, they're on their own. No more counseling. No telephone calls. No support should they falter. Necessarily, then, the rates of success in the regular population are typically less than those in a study population.

Think about this example. Say you go to the sporting goods store and buy a pair of roller blades. You've always wanted to learn how to roller blade. You pick out a nice pair, go to the cashier, and make your purchase. As you leave the store, the sales associate pulls you to the side and talks to you for five minutes about how to roller blade. You're told to put your feet into the skates this way, then lace them up that way, then stand this way, and push off that way. After these five minutes of instruction, you proceed home. You pull into your driveway, jump out of your car, open your trunk, and pull out your new roller blades. You put your feet in, lace them up, stand up, and push off, just as the sales associate instructed. Now what? You're speeding down the street without a clue as to what to do next. How do you turn? How do you stop? How do you prevent yourself from hitting that tree in front of you? You'd probably take your roller blades off and put them in the closet before you hurt yourself.

Now say you leave the sporting goods store with the sales associate. You arrive at your home, jump out of the car, and lace up your skates. The sales associate hoists you up, stands next to you, and instructs you in detail on how to push off, stop, turn, speed up, and slow down. After one hour of intense, personal instruction, the sales associate leaves, telling you that he'll be back tomorrow for more instruction. And so, the two of you work to hone your skating skills daily for three weeks. After that three week period, he calls you weekly for a whole year to monitor your success and to see if you have any questions. By the end of this period, you'd likely be an expert skater.

You, as a member of the regular population trying to quit smoking, need to understand this difference. A given intervention may work wonderfully for someone whose abstinence is supported and reinforced by a large network of supporters and instructors. However, if you're alone in your quest to quit smoking, and all you have to work with is a little pill in your hand, or a patch on your arm, or a piece of gum in your mouth, you may not achieve quite the same degree of success. There are two solutions to this problem. First, you can enroll yourself in a behavioral and cognitive therapy program geared toward smoking cessation. They do exist outside of research studies, and are quite effective. Second, you can motivate yourself to the extent that you become your own counselor, instructor, and critic. Use the methods we've discussed in this book to guide yourself toward cessation. Make yourself responsible to yourself. Feel disappointed if you smoke another cigarette. Reward yourself if you succeed at quitting. Address your triggers and find solutions to beat them. Make yourself more like those in the study population, and you'll come closer to achieving their degree of success.

Next, you need to realize the difference between a relative benefit and an absolute benefit. I stated earlier that people taking Zyban were twice as likely to stop smoking as those not taking it. That sounds great, right. By taking Zyban, you double your chances to quit. However, I failed to mention how many people actually stopped smoking. Actually, one year after completing their courses of Zyban, only thirty-six percent of smokers remained free from cigarettes. Sixty-four percent of them returned to smoking within one year. Well now, that doesn't sound too good. Where does the discrepancy lie? In this situation, the relative benefit sounds promising, in that you're twice as likely to quit using Zyban. However, the absolute benefit is small, in that you only have a thirty-six percent chance of being free from cigarettes after one year. In actuality, no matter what you do, the chances of success at smoking cessation are small, and if you double something small, you still have something small. If you double the size of an ant, you still have a small insect. Even if you double your chances of winning the lottery, your chances still are slim. So while these medications and nicotine replacement therapies work well when compared to taking nothing, their overall benefit remains small.

Third, as you see, we have the recurrent issue of risk versus benefit, which we have discussed above in the context of use of clonidine, but which applies to any medication you may choose to use for smoking cessation. No medication is truly without side effects. Even vitamins you purchase in a drug store have side effects if you take too much of them. And some side effects can be quite serious; refer especially to our discussion of nortriptyline for some potentially bad side effects. Consider the real possibility of these unfortunate occurrences when judging your options for smoking cessation.

Fourth, no matter which method you choose, it will never replace a true will to quit. As we've mentioned before, in order to quit, you have to want to quit. Many people, lacking a true desire to quit, choose one of these medications, thinking that it will make them quit. They use them as crutches, trying to substitute a quick-fix for a true long-term commitment. Let's use crutches as an example, shall we? Say you sprain your ankle, and you need to use crutches to get around. You still need to exert some effort, right. You need to swing your leg, pick up the crutches and move them forward, and bear your weight on your good leg. The crutches only help you to walk, they don't carry you around. The same idea applies to these nicotine replacement therapies and medications as crutches. Use them as supplements to your cessation attempt, not as their replacement.

Given all of this, the question remains as to which agent, if any, to use. Well, we discussed one agent that you should definitely not try, and quite a few that you are free to try as long as you understand the potential risks and side effects we discussed. With this information in mind, try whatever you want. If you don't mind taking pills, discuss one of the medications with your doctor. If you'd rather proceed non-medicinally, choose one of the nicotine replacement agents. If you fail with one regimen, try another. They have definite efficacy, and may just help you to quit for good.

What About Alternatives?

There are always choices in life. 7-Up or Sprite? Car or SUV? Left or right? Blue or red? Life is full of choices, options, alternatives. And as a smoker trying to quit, you also have options. In addition to the methods that I espouse, there are alternative modes of quitting. For the sake of completeness, we will review these techniques together, with one caveat. I won't merely mention them to you for your reading enjoyment. I'll mention them, describe them, and then reveal objective literature that tells us if they work or not. Granted, individual circumstances exist, and you'll easily find people who have succeeded using any of the methods we will discuss. However, it's always helpful to know ahead of time which ones are more likely to work than others; that way, if you attempt one of these alternative systems, you'll have a greater chance to succeed. I want you to stop smoking; I don't want you to waste your time.

Acupuncture

Acupuncture, a branch of traditional Chinese medicine, has been a practice since ancient times, possibly started as much as four thousand years ago. Despite this long history, studded with many treatment successes, the traditional and alternative medical communities still don't really know how it works. The concept of acupuncture suggests that energy currents circulate in channels throughout the body, from head to toe and from left to right, in a finely coordinated dance. Also within these channels travels the life force. These channels are called "meridians", and each organ in the body has its own meridian. In order for a person to be healthy, the currents within these meridia must flow in a balanced fashion throughout the entire body. If one of these meridia is disrupted, illness occurs. The purpose of acupuncture, then, is to restore proper current flow through the meridia. In the beginning, practitioners of acupuncture used sharpened stones to reprogram the meridia. Nowadays, they accomplish this by inserting a needle into the meridian that corresponds to an individual's given illness. Points within these meridia are mapped, and there are about 354 different points on the body. Sometimes, practitioners of acupuncture will burn an herb called moxa directly onto the skin along the meridia, or at the end of a short needle inserted into the meridia; this is thought to be effective in actually preventing disease. In other situations, acupuncturists will send a small electric current through the needles into the skin, again hoping to correct a misalignment of the meridian in question. In modern times, the main utility of acupuncture is in the relief of pain. Acupuncture has also been shown effective in the treatment of nausea after surgery.

Modern acupuncture techniques have focused on ear acupuncture; practitioners in France began to tout this method in the 20th century. According to acupuncture lore, all of the meridia meet at the ears, thereby giving the acupuncturist access to the entire body. Also, acupuncturists liken the outer ear to a fetus in a womb positioned upside-down, such that the earlobe would correspond to the head. Therefore, an acupuncturist can theoretically treat most conditions by concentrating on the meridia within the outer ear alone. For example, you would treat a headache by concentrating on placing needles in the earlobe, and you would treat back pain by positioning needles along the inner aspect of the ear, in the middle.

There are three points along the outer edge of the outer ear, right along the rim, that hold relevance for smoking cessation. Some acupuncturists will place needles into these points for a short period of time, with or without electric input, over a period of several sessions. Others will place more long-term needles, called staples, into these points in an attempt to address cigarette cravings in real time. A smoker will press on these staples whenever he or she experiences a craving. Still others have identified points on the face that hold import for smoking cessation.

But does acupuncture work for smoking cessation? Well, yes and no. In trials, acupuncture has been tested against sham, or fake, acupuncture. Sham acupuncture involves placing needles on the skin which stay in place without piercing the skin, and thereby theoretically not affecting the meridia. Many studies, involving thousands of people, have been performed comparing acupuncture to fake acupuncture, as well as to other smoking cessation techniques. Across the board, studies have failed to demonstrate any appreciable benefit from acupuncture for those wishing to quit smoking. In other words, people were no more likely to be successful quitting smoking with acupuncture than with sham acupuncture.

But why, then, are some people successful quitting smoking with acupuncture? I'm sure you've heard of someone who went for acupuncture and hasn't smoked a single cigarette since. Why was that person able to stop? Why did acupuncture work for him or her? To understand this, we need to discuss the concept of bias. If you look at the studies on acupuncture for smoking cessation, you'll notice that the same percentage of people who tried acupuncture quit smoking as those who had sham acupuncture. However, compared to those receiving no acupuncture whatsoever, people in the real and sham acupuncture groups quit more often. This means that having some intervention was better than having no intervention, regardless of the type of intervention. When the study participants received some intervention, be it real or fake, they felt more empowered than if they received nothing, because they felt that something was being done. And something is better than nothing. Not knowing whether their intervention was real or fake, people were more likely to quit simply because they felt that they were receiving something. We call this the placebo effect, a bias that affects studies in traditional and alternative medicine alike. This is akin to someone stating that his or her pain improved from an injection of water after being told that the water was actually pain medication; the pain improved because the person expected it to improve, thinking that he or she was getting pain medication. This is why researchers needed to compare real acupuncture to sham acupuncture. Comparing an intervention to no intervention would have given a false impression that the intervention worked. But by comparing two interventions, one real and one fake, they were able to demonstrate that the real intervention was no better than the fake one. In this way, they were truly able to show that, overall, acupuncture does not work for smoking cessation. Individuals may experience benefit because they expect to. They may stop smoking because they expect acupuncture to work, because they expect to be able to stop.

Acupuncture has been in practice for many millenia, and traditional and alternative practitioners still don't know how it actually works. What we do know, however, is that, in and of itself, acupuncture may not work for smoking cessation. No trials have demonstrated that real acupuncture works better than fake acupuncture. The chief success of acupuncture in the context of smoking cessation lies solely in the placebo effect. But in actuality, when compared to receiving nothing, undergoing acupuncture, be it real of fake, does improve your chances of quitting smoking; in this context, the benefit of this placebo effect cannot be denied. So whether or not current flow through your meridia is truly being restored, you're quitting, which is the ultimate goal anyway. So it may be worth your while to try acupuncture. If you have a real desire to stop smoking, acupuncture may represent the trigger you need to throw away your cigarettes for good.

Hypnosis

There are two schools of thought as to the development of hypnosis. The first dates back to the fourteenth century, when healers taught that illness represented a punishment from the gods. These healers would induce a state of profound calm in their patients, through music, chanting, or even drugs. After their patients achieved a trance-like state of relaxation, the healers would feed them suggestions of cure. Patients would believe that they were being healed; this is what we now call the "power or suggestion." The healers attempted to infuse their suggestions into their patients' subconscious minds during this state of relaxation, thereby letting their patients' own mind power cure them. People would feel better because they believed they were going to feel better. Widespread employment of this technique began in the Sleep Temples of Egypt, in which people would congregate to be treated by these healers.

The second school of thought dates back to the sixteenth century, and the work of Paracelsus, who touted that the heavens exerted an influence on health and disease through a universal magnetic field. The work of Paracelsus was put into practice in the eighteenth century by Dr. Franz Anton Mesmer (think mesmerized), who stated that all people have a universal magnetic fluid flowing through them which joins them to each other, the environment, the heavens, and all animals and plants. According to his theory, cures could be achieved through affecting this magnetic fluid. He would place patients into a state of profound relaxation, then place magnets on their bodies in an attempt to induce a cure of illness by restoring proper magnetic flow. In fact, in his heyday, he would submerse several people at once in large pots filled with water and magnets. And he was very successful; many people claimed to have been cured by Dr. Mesmer and his magnets. However, when the practice of Dr. Mesmer was scrutinized, it was discovered that the placement of magnets on the body was far less important than the achievement of a deep state of relaxation. Once again, the power of suggestion came to the forefront.

Concentration on the achievement of profound relaxation began with the work of Dr. James Braid in the nineteenth century, who first coined the term "hypnosis" to describe this state of near sleep. He declared that the state of hypnosis occurs after a period of intense concentration which would leave the patient completely fatigued; this fatigue then left patients suggestible. He would have his patients stare intently at a bright object until they nearly fell asleep, then would feed them suggestions of cure. The work of Dr. Braid opened the doors for the modern practice of hypnotherapy.

Today, hypnotherapy is used in many contexts, including smoking cessation, sleep disorders, overeating, anorexia, and even for asthma and frequent urination. In fact, people can even participate in self-hypnosis, in which they place themselves into a trance-like state through meditation, then feed themselves positive thoughts. Hypnosis for smoking cessation focuses on combating withdrawal symptoms with positive thoughts that discount them. Suggestive thoughts in this context imply, for example, that cigarette smoke tastes terrible, or that cessation will help you be healthy. Through these suggestive thoughts, the hypnotist can make you completely change your mind about your desire to smoke; he or she can make you absolutely hate cigarettes. For example, after the hypnotist places you into a state of profound relaxation, he or she may tell you things like, "Smelling cigarette smoke will make you nauseous." You can even tell yourself this during a period of self-hypnosis. The thoughts would, theoretically, enter your subconscious mind and influence your conscious thoughts the next time you encounter a cigarette, when you would truly feel nauseous. You would, thereby, develop a true aversion to cigarettes, making cessation much easier.

But does hypnotherapy truly work for smoking cessation? It all depends on who you believe. The traditional medical community will tell you that no concrete evidence exists to support the efficacy of hypnotherapy for smoking cessation. This is because the process of hypnosis lacks evaluation by controlled trials. Research is considered controlled when two groups of people are matched on every possible variable except for one, which is being studied. By performing controlled trials, researchers attempt to prove that this one variable is responsible for the differences between the two groups. For example, say you want to determine if people can throw a tennis ball farther than a basketball in an open field. As a researcher, you would need to create two groups of people, those who will throw the tennis ball and those who will throw the basketball. Then, you would need to match every other factor between the groups except for the type of ball being thrown. You would need the same number of men and women, the same average age, the same average strength, the same degree of coordination, the same wind speed, and so on. This way, you could truly compare which ball can be thrown farther, because the only uncontrolled variable would be the characteristics of the balls themselves. Now, say the average age of the tennis ball throwers is eighteen years, and that of the basketball throwers is eighty years. Given this, you may not be able to tell if the tennis balls are thrown farther because of the characteristics of the balls themselves, or because the younger people in that group are able to throw any type of ball farther that the older people in the basketball group. In this case, age would be an uncontrolled variable that might skew your results.

Also, to make a study truly valid, it should be blinded as to which form of the uncontrolled variable each individual receives. Basically, this means that, in our example, each person wouldn't know if they were throwing a tennis ball or a basketball. In this way, since your subjects wouldn't know which ball they're throwing, you avoid the imposition of subjectivity.

Now, since there are scarce controlled studies on the effects of hypnotherapy on smoking cessation, the traditional medical community calls hypnotherapy ineffective for this purpose. But how can you truly perform a controlled, blinded trial of hypnosis? On the one hand, you can't control an individual's receptiveness to hypnosis. Hypnotists cite several methods available to determine an individual's ability to be hypnotized, but too much subjectivity exists in the actual experience of hypnosis to be able to control every possible variable. On the other hand, it's impossible to blind a trial of hypnosis; you can't fake hypnosis-either you're being hypnotized or you're not. Study subjects would obviously know if they're being hypnotized or not, so you could never perform a blinded trial of hypnotherapy.

Despite the traditional medical community's insistence on the inefficacy of hypnotherapy for smoking cessation, hypnotists will cite very high rates of success, even after only one session. That's because they perform many uncontrolled studies proving their effectiveness. They do this by simply following their subjects after their hypnotherapy sessions to see if and when they start smoking again. Performing uncontrolled studies eliminates the need for control and blinding. However, it leaves the potential for your results to be explained by another mechanism, like the ball throwing example we discussed above. Nevertheless, hypnotists acknowledge success rates as high as ninety percent after their smoking cessation sessions. Furthermore, their results are often durable over time. So, to answer the question, hypnotherapy does seem to work for smoking cessation.

Exercise

Everyone should be exercising, whether they're smokers or not. Exercise lowers your cholesterol, strengthens your heart, controls your weight, burns calories, and helps you live longer. And luckily, exercise helps you quit smoking. Research has shown that people who exercise while trying to quit smoking are more likely to quit. Furthermore, they are more likely to remain free of cigarettes for at least one year.

There are several benefits of exercise in your smoking cessation plan. For one, smoking cessation and exercise can be clumped together in a total body health plan. Stopping smoking, like exercise, is good for you. You can combine the two with, for example, removing fast food from your diet as a complete plan for health. In this way, you can envision yourself as a completely healthy person rather than as a completely unhealthy person. You exercise, you eat right, and you don't smoke. You're a health nut. Grouping smoking cessation with other healthy behaviors will actually help you abstain from cigarettes, because smoking will make you feel unhealthy. This employs the power of imagery that we have discussed in a previous chapter.

Second, exercise can distract you from the cravings of nicotine withdrawal. Say you awaken in the morning with a strong craving for a cigarette. Well, put on your jogging outfit and sneakers and go for a run. Say you're craving a cigarette during the drive home from work. Turn around and go to the gym for a work-out. You can use exercise in this way to effectively suppress your cravings for nicotine.

Third, and most importantly for some, exercise has been shown to reduce or eliminate the weight gain associated with smoking cessation. After stopping smoking, people can expect to gain an average of five or ten pounds. Some people gain much more weight. This has been attributed to an individual's need for a replacement for the hand-to-mouth action they're accustomed to as smokers, substituting food for a cigarette. Also, people often use food to distract themselves from cravings. Exercising will abate or obviate this weight gain.

So get yourself involved in an exercise regimen. It will help you quit smoking, and will keep your weight in check. Best of all, it will promote your overall health and extend your life.

Herbs

Herbs have been used for medicinal purposes since prehistoric times. Drawings in caves detail the use of herbs by cavemen. Historically, Greeks, Romans, Chinese, and Egyptians have used herbs extensively to treat various conditions. In fact, the Egyptians had over seven hundred herbal preparations over three thousand years ago. And books were written outlining the use of specific herbs to treat specific illnesses as early as the first century. Today, there are hundreds if not thousands of herbs, used individually or in combination to treat illness.

The herb mentioned in the context of smoking cessation is lobelia. Lobelia is a perennial herb that typically grows in the northern United States and in Canada. It stands one to three feet in height, and bears scarlet, purple, or blue flowers, sometimes mixed with patches of white, in the late summer to early fall.

Although is prefers partial shade, lobelia also grows well in full sun with moist soil. As ornamental plants, they can be used to edge flower beds, or can be planted in hanging baskets.

When the leaves of lobelia are ground, a greenish powder is produced. This powder contains a substance called lobeline. Lobeline is an herb that has been recommended as an expectorant, diuretic, and anti-asthmatic preparation. It has also been used variably for epilepsy, tetanus, and tonsilitis. Externally, it has been used on cuts and bruises.

The FDA has cautioned as to the use of lobeline. In large doses, lobeline can cause vomiting, a characteristic that has been sometimes useful medicinally. Additionally, after ingestion, lobeline can cause diarrhea, vision and hearing difficulties, confusion, dangerously low blood pressure, and difficulty breathing. Death has occurred from overdoses of lobeline.

Lobeline has been touted for smoking cessation because it binds to the same receptors in the brain as nicotine. By binding to these receptors, lobeline can block the effects of nicotine on the brain. Additionally, lobeline mimics nicotine somewhat and therefore can theoretically activate these nicotine receptors to a small degree. Since the nicotine receptors are being activated by lobeline, your brain, in concept, would not miss nicotine after you stop smoking, and so your withdrawal symptoms and cravings would be minimized. It's like switching from regular to low-fat peanut butter. You can still make a peanut butter and jelly sandwich, but it's just not the same.

So, does lobeline work for smoking cessation? Unfortunately, no. No good study on the topic has shown lobeline to be effective in helping people stop smoking. Furthermore, as we've discussed above, lobeline can be dangerous; overdose can even lead to death. So not only would it not help you to quit smoking, but it can cause you serious health concerns. So plant it in your garden, but don't take it for smoking cessation.

Summary

The treatment options we've discussed here are considered alternative because they fall outside the realm of traditional medicine. But this doesn't necessarily mean that they are inferior to traditional medicine. The fact is that some of these methods may help you quit smoking, and sometimes can be even more effective than traditional medicine. Remember, while the best medical regimen for smoking cessation achieves a success rate of about thirty-five percent, hypnotists claim rates of success as high as ninety percent. So don't discount these methods of smoking cessation en bloc, despite what traditional research suggests. We may not understand why they work, but sometimes they do.

Before we close this discussion, I need to mention some precautions governing the use of alternative medicine strategies in general. First of all, alternative strategies are not necessarily harmless. Let's talk about herbs, for example. People tend to regard alternatives such as herbs as harmless; if they don't work, at least they're not dangerous, right? Unfortunately, the use of herbs can be very dangerous, and even life-threatening. You need to realize that herbs are medicinal, and can therefore have adverse effects just like medications. St John's Wort, for one, is similar to a class of antidepressants called MAO inhibitors, named for the enzyme in the brain that they inhibit; this is why they work as antidepressants. However, St. John's Wort also shares the same side effects as the rest of the MAO inhibitors, and can cause serious adverse consequences if combined with other antidepressants. Another herb, ma huang, has been touted as an effective weight loss agent. Ma huang mimics the stimulant hormones that occur within us naturally, such as adrenaline. However, ma huang has also been documented to cause heart rhythm disturbances and sudden death, even when used in regularly recommended doses; you don't even need to overdose on the stuff for it to kill you. So please don't regard herbs as harmless choices; they can be very harmful.

Second, don't discount the placebo effect. I know we discussed this effect negatively because it masks an apparent lack of benefit of a given smoking cessation method, such as acupuncture. However, we discuss the placebo effect in the context of a population of people who are exposed to the given intervention. You are an individual, with your own characteristics, beliefs, and motives. Individual successes have been documented with all of these alternative strategies, whether or not the strategy has been definitively shown to work for the population in general. In this sense, an individual's belief system comes into play. If someone truly believes in the efficacy of acupuncture, for example, he or she would likely be successful at quitting smoking via acupuncture, regardless of what the popular press has to say about its effectiveness. The power of optimism leads to success. In this way, you could pour a glass of water, squeeze some lime juice into it, and promote it as a smoking cessation aid; if you promote it strongly enough, and if you convince enough people that this glass of lime water will help them quit smoking, you'll sell your product. Furthermore, a good number of those people who purchased your lime water will drink it diligently, and will actually quit smoking, because you've made them believe that this simple glass of lime water will help them quit. Their optimism about your product, this glass of water, will drive them to cessation success. Remember, ultimately, you want to stop smoking, and if a placebo will help you to stop, then use the placebo.

Third, realize that these strategies will not replace a true desire to stop smoking. Like medications and nicotine replacement methods, people often turn to these alternatives to make them stop smoking. They try to use these methods to replace their lack of a true desire to stop smoking. The fact is that none of these strategies will make you stop smoking; only you will make you stop smoking. If you have a true desire to stop, these techniques can assist you in the achievement of that goal, but they will not work in the absence of a true commitment to quit.

Finally, keep an open mind, and trust your own instincts. Without an open mind, we may never have isolated penicillin from mold. We may never have discovered that we can travel to outer space. We may not have invented automobiles, airplanes, computers, dishwashers, or microwave ovens. Likewise, these alternatives may work if you remain receptive to their potential efficacy. Don't rule them out simply because they seem different; they just might work for you.

What To Expect When You Stop

Before you throw out those cigarettes and attempt to quit smoking, you need to understand what to expect in terms of withdrawal. The main substance referred to in the context of cigarette dependence and withdrawal symptoms is nicotine, which we have discussed previously. The more nicotine you inhale in the course of a day, the more severe the withdrawal symptoms you can expect to experience. As a rule of thumb, people who smoke more than twenty-five cigarettes each day, and those who smoke their first cigarette within thirty minutes of awakening in the morning will have severe symptoms of withdrawal. Also, for each cigarette smoked, those who smoke cigarettes with higher nicotine content can expect more severe symptoms. However, even people who smoke very little can expect some degree of withdrawal; no smoker will have a symptom-free quit attempt. Unfortunately, the easiest way to abort withdrawal symptoms is to smoke a cigarette-obviously counter-productive when your goal is to stop smoking. Therefore, understanding the symptoms of withdrawal, and developing methods (other than smoking) for the reduction and tolerance of these symptoms, will help you to prevent relapsing into smoking behavior. We will discuss both physical and psychological withdrawal symptoms, then work through means to reduce or eliminate their influence on your quit attempt, thereby maximizing your chance for success.

Physical Withdrawal

Physical withdrawal occurs because your body becomes used to functioning in the presence of nicotine. The more nicotine you inhale during the course of days, weeks, and years, the more ingrained that nicotine becomes in the daily functioning of your body. The sudden removal of that large amount of nicotine will disrupt your body's ability to function normally for about two or three weeks. Until your body re-programs itself to function without nicotine, you'll feel withdrawal symptoms. To give you an example, speak to someone who has had their gall bladder removed. The gall bladder is involved in the digestion of fat from our meals. When your gall bladder is removed, it becomes difficult for your body to digest fat; after a fatty meal, you would feel very bloated and uncomfortable. If you speak to someone who has had their gall bladder removed, they'll tell you that after they started to eat normally again, they felt very uncomfortable after eating, especially if the meal had a high fat content. However, they'll likely tell you that after a while, the discomfort went away. After your gall bladder is removed for some time, the body adjusts itself, and learns how to digest fats adequately without a gall bladder. Same rules apply for nicotine. Initially, you will feel discomfort as your body functions without nicotine, but eventually your body will learn to work without it, and the physical withdrawal symptoms will resolve. Your short-term goal in this context is to prevent yourself from smoking while letting these symptoms run their course. Returning to smoking will eliminate your discomfort, but will ruin your quit attempt.

One symptom you will experience is an intense craving for a cigarette. As we will discuss in a later chapter, your brain wants you to continue smoking. Your brain will send strong signals to you urging you to smoke again. This will likely be the first withdrawal symptom you'll feel; nicotine lasts in your body only for two or three hours, so you will feel this craving two to three hours after your last cigarette. If you smoke your last cigarette on the night before your quit date, you'll likely awaken in the morning with an intense craving for a cigarette. Luckily, these cravings only last a couple of minutes each. Further, they will probably stop by the third day of your quit attempt.

Related to these cravings, nicotine withdrawal also results in irritability. You'll feel very anxious and restless. You may even become angry and snap at people at work or home. This anxiety results from the internal conflict inherent in strongly wanting something you know you shouldn't have-a cigarette.

Another withdrawal symptom is the inability to concentrate and pay attention to tasks. Remember, among other things, cigarettes help you to focus and concentrate. Smokers feel more alert after they've smoked a cigarette. This is, again, due to the influence of nicotine on your brain; nicotine floods the pathways in your brain that are responsible for wakefulness and attention. Without nicotine, you'll feel unable to concentrate, your mind will wander, and you'll be easily distracted.

Along this line, nicotine withdrawal will also leave you feeling fatigued and listless. Without the large amounts of nicotine that once pummeled your brain with signals promoting wakefulness, you'll feel very tired during the day. Remember, a cigarette is usually the "pick-me-up" that gets you through a grueling day. Without it, you'll tire more easily.

Yet another withdrawal symptom you may experience, the one that is most feared by many, is weight gain. Nicotine is an appetite suppressant; removal of nicotine from your system may cause intense hunger. With hunger may come increased eating, and with increased eating will come weight gain. This possibility alone causes many to fear smoking cessation, as they expect to gain huge amounts of weight once they stop smoking. Actually, the amount of weight typically gained is about five to ten pounds.

Other symptoms that you may experience are headache, cough, depression, and dizziness. These, too, have to do with the acute removal of nicotine from a body that has grown to require it for normal functioning. Like the other symptoms mentioned, these should only last a few weeks. However, during those few weeks, you are at very high risk to resume smoking. You'll know in your mind that all you need to do is smoke a cigarette and all these symptoms will go away. In this situation, don't fool yourself into thinking you'll be able to just smoke one cigarette to remove the symptoms. Some people, especially when their symptoms become unbearable, will smoke one cigarette to give themselves some relief from their withdrawal symptoms. Granted, this does work, but only temporarily. Remember, nicotine only lasts in your system for two or three hours. After this period of time, withdrawal symptoms will predictably return. Once your withdrawal symptoms continuously overwhelm you, and you keep smoking cigarettes to ease them, you've become a smoker again. Your goal is to develop methods to combat these withdrawal symptoms, so you can control them without returning to smoking.

Psychological Withdrawal

Psychological withdrawal is an intangible dependence on cigarette smoking that prevents you from quitting, and that can continue to function long after your physical withdrawal symptoms have dissipated. While physical withdrawal occurs because of nicotine's effects in your body, psychological withdrawal results from the effects of smoking on your life. Cigarettes likely play a role in some of your happiest memories. You may have smoked at the high school prom, at the World Series, at your wedding, and when you bought your first car. You may have bought your first pack of cigarettes with your best friend, and have fond memories of smoking that first cigarette with him or her in the playground after school. You remember being on vacation, sitting on a beach, drinking a margarita, and smoking a cigarette. While you understand objectively that you need to stop smoking, subjectively you feel attached to cigarettes because of these associations with happy occurrences. In this context, it's very difficult to dissociate the cigarettes from those happy thoughts, so smoking behavior is continued because it evokes happiness. Why would you want to stop doing something that makes you feel happy? The basis of managing psychological withdrawal, then, is to replace the positive associations of cigarettes with negative ones, such as the health and social ills we've discussed previously. When you can mentally and emotionally classify cigarettes as negative rather than positive, you'll be prepared to defeat psychological dependence.

Research has definitively proven that nicotine is psychologically addictive. Evidence suggestive of a deep dependence on nicotine, and therefore a good chance of experiencing psychological withdrawal, include smoking high-nicotine cigarettes, smoking more than twenty-five cigarettes per day, smoking in the early morning upon awakening, and feeling discomfort when in a non-smoking environment. Think about this. I told you before that nicotine lasts in your system for two to three hours. Let's be as conservative as possible and figure that because of the development of physical withdrawal symptoms, you need to smoke every two hours. That equates to twelve cigarettes, at most, in the course of a day that can be accounted for by physical dependence. Now we all know that some smokers go through up to four packs per day, and it's not unusual to find smokers who exhaust two packs per day. Since we've already figured out that these cigarettes are not needed for symptoms of physical withdrawal, they must serve some purpose for the reduction of psychological withdrawal. Therefore, you'll never kick your smoking habit until you defeat both your physical and psychological dependence.

The danger of psychological withdrawal is its intangibility. No laboratory value or vital sign measurement of X-ray will tell you that you're psychologically dependent on cigarettes. Evidence for such is hidden deep within your brain, in the centers for emotion and enjoyment. Later in this book, you will discover how nicotine activates centers in your brain that signal reward for a given behavior; your brain actually rewards you for smoking, and helps to establish psychological dependence to nicotine. While you can easily determine if a physical symptom has gone away, it's more difficult to ascertain whether or not your brain is sending you the wrong message about your smoking behavior, promoting it when it should be discouraging it. In order to overcome psychological dependence, you need to defeat yourself, so to speak. In other words, you need to convince your brain that it's wrong. You need to convince your brain that smoking cigarettes is wrong.

Summary

Now that you understand the bases of both physical and psychological withdrawal, we will discuss methods to combat both. One important difference between the two that you must understand before we proceed is the time line of the two. While physical withdrawal lasts only a few weeks, psychological withdrawal can last for years, even forever. So while you can truly defeat physical dependence, you can only hope to control psychological dependence. With that in mind, let's proceed.

One way to reduce the symptoms of physical withdrawal is easy-give yourself nicotine. Yes, I know, I just told you not to smoke when you feel withdrawal symptoms. What I mean is nicotine replacement therapy, which works very well for the physical symptoms of withdrawal. There are several types of nicotine replacement, which we will discuss later in this book. Logic would tell you that if your body is suffering because of a lack of nicotine, you can feel better by replacing that nicotine-as we said before, that's why many smokers revert to smoking during this period of withdrawal. Instead of choosing cigarettes, though, you can choose from patches, gums, inhalers, and lozenges. The benefit of using nicotine replacement is that your physical withdrawal symptoms will be lessened, eliminating the chance of them causing you to revert to smoking. Furthermore, nicotine replacement methods allow you to concentrate more of your efforts on battling your symptoms of psychological withdrawal, the methods for which we will discuss in a bit. One problem with nicotine replacement is that you can actually become addicted to the nicotine replacement agent if you're not careful. You may find yourself chewing twenty-eight pieces of gum each day, or wearing eighteen nicotine patches at once. By using them in this fashion, you're merely substituting one addiction for another. Now, granted, nicotine replacement agents are still safer than cigarettes in that they don't contain those carcinogens that we find in cigarettes. However, the utility of the agents should be to assist you in toppling your addiction, not continuing your addiction in a different form. You wouldn't try to conquer an addiction to marijuana by smoking crack, would you? Another problem with nicotine replacement agents is that they do not actively address psychological addiction. So your work toward quitting is definitely not done once you slap that patch onto your shoulder; you still actively need to address your psychological dependence. Overall, when used properly, nicotine replacement agents can be very useful during the two to three week period of physical withdrawal.

Another way to reduce the effects of physical withdrawal is through the art of distraction. You need to engage yourself in some activity that diverts your attention from the physical discomfort you're feeling. This technique has tremendous utility in the face of cravings. Remember, cravings only last a few minutes at a time. If you're able to distract yourself for those few minutes, you'll allow the craving to pass without giving in to it. I'll give you an example. You wake up in the morning, go to the kitchen and brew yourself some coffee. As you sit at the kitchen table with your cup of coffee in front of you, a sudden craving overcomes you. You would love to light up a cigarette right now and smoke it with your cup of coffee. Instead, however, you jump up from your seat, leave your coffee on the table, run to the bathroom, and jump into the shower. You can't smoke while you're in the shower, right? You've officially distracted yourself. By the time you finish your shower, your craving will have passed, and you will have avoided smoking a cigarette. Get dressed, go back to the kitchen, pop that cold cup of coffee in the microwave, and congratulate yourself.

I'll give you another example. You're sitting on your couch at the end of a long day. You've exercised, you've eaten a good dinner, and you're on that couch watching prime-time television. And here comes a craving. You'd love to kick back on the couch and smoke a cigarette right now. But instead, you get up, walk over to your computer and check your e-mail (or if you don't have a computer, go check your regular mail). That craving should pass before you've finished sifting through your junk mail. When you're finished, jump back onto that couch and kick back, thrilled with the fact that you just avoided another cigarette.

So you see, through the art of distraction, you can allow cravings to pass. Just one quick hint about the distractions you choose-try to choose distractions that fit with your personality and your lifestyle. Only you can decide what distractions will work for you. As a silly example, I'll tell you that the next time you feel a craving, open a newspaper and complete the daily crossword puzzle. Now some of you may love crossword puzzles, and would see this as a great idea. However, some of you may hate crossword puzzles, and having to work on one would cause you so much stress that you'd be even more likely to grab a cigarette and start smoking just for the stress relief. Your distractions should be things you enjoy, things you would be happy to do. A hobby is a perfect distraction-paint a picture, build a birdhouse, plant a tree. Choose anything that you will enjoy, and that will take your attention away from the craving for cigarettes.

Before moving on to psychological withdrawal, I need to comment on the issue of weight gain and smoking cessation. Again, nicotine acts as an appetite suppressant, and withdrawal from smoking can lead to intense hunger, increased eating, and weight gain. On average, smokers gain about ten pounds overall after stopping smoking. But this is not a guarantee. You can easily prevent the weight gain associated with smoking cessation. For one, if you feel you have to eat, choose healthy food choices. As opposed to cigarette cravings, food cravings usually last until you eat something; you're unlikely to be able to distract yourself from a craving for food. If you need to eat something to satisfy that craving, choose a food that's good for you, like a piece of fruit or a cup of vegetables. Second, it's been well established in the medical literature that exercise can prevent the weight gain associated with smoking cessation. Specifically, you need to engage in aerobic activity, such as walking, cycling, or swimming. So to avoid the weight gain associated with quitting smoking, eat right and exercise. Gee, you should be doing that anyway.

As far as psychological withdrawal is concerned, the main technique you can employ is a repeat of one used previously-positive reinforcement. Always remember that you had excellent reasons to stop smoking. You need to maintain confidence in the fact that you did the right thing by quitting, despite the happy memories you associate with cigarette smoking. You're making yourself a healthier person. You'll live longer. You'll be able to do more in your day without getting winded or coughing uncontrollably. Congratulate yourself often for your success. Be happy with yourself for having quit. Remember, your brain is trying to tell you that smoking is good; you need to convince your brain that cessation is good. Preserve a positive outlook toward smoking cessation, rather than toward smoking, and you're more likely to remain an ex-smoker.

Another technique you can employ to combat psychological withdrawal is to create your own support group, so to speak. Collect a list of friends and relatives who are non-smokers or ex-smokers, and tell them that you've quit smoking. For one, their enthusiasm will provide more positive reinforcement for your decision to quit. Also, by telling people who have quit smoking in the past that you, too, have quit smoking, you will enlist a group of allies who will watch over you and help you to achieve long-lasting success. If you're at a function together, they'll likely watch over you to make sure you don't pull out a cigarette. If you feel uncontrollable urges to smoke, you can call one of them and ask them to work you through the craving. You'll surely have ample opportunity to return their favors; remember, quitting smoking is difficult for everyone.

Most importantly, remember that psychological dependence acts forever. Since memories last forever, your association between cigarettes and happy memories may last forever. People who return to smoking years after they've quit have been defeated by their psychological dependence; they've given in to the lure of making more happy memories as a smoker. Therefore, don't expect to overcome psychological withdrawal with a quick fix. You must battle psychological withdrawal constantly, daily, forever. It becomes easier to manage if you accept that this battle will be, in fact, life-long. Once you lighten your defenses against psychological dependence, even if you haven't smoked for years, you put yourself at risk for relapsing to smoking.

In conclusion, accept that withdrawal will happen. Every smoker who quits will experience some degree of withdrawal. Your task is to know what physical symptoms to expect before they happen, and to develop strategies to fight them away. Also, you need to accept the power and longevity of psychological withdrawal, and commit your life to suppressing it. Prepare yourself for the fight, and you'll win the fight.

Don't Worry-You're Going To Fail

Back in Chapter Six, I neglected to tell you about one possible stage of smoking cessation, *relapse*. Relapse happens if maintenance doesn't. You relapse when you return to smoking after you have quit for a period of time. You can enact your smoking cessation plan with the best intentions and strongest convictions, and still relapse. And relapse is failure.

As disheartening as this sounds, it's unfortunately true. If you've already tried to stop smoking, or if you know someone who has tried, you know this is true. In fact, it takes the average smoker seven attempts to finally quit smoking. And what's worse, you can fail at any time after you've quit. You can last a week, or a year, or a decade without a single cigarette then, regretfully, return to smoking. Disheartening, but true.

But why do people fail? Why can't you just throw out your cigarettes and be done with it?

Enjoyment

Well, for one, people usually smoke because they enjoy smoking. Sounds logical, right? But this is one of the most important reasons why people fail to quit so often. Why would you want to stop doing something you enjoy so much? If you didn't enjoy smoking, you would have stopped on your own a long time ago. Think about it. If you don't enjoy skiing, you don't sign up for ski trips. If you don't like Neil Diamond, you don't buy his CDs. And if you didn't enjoy smoking, you wouldn't be smoking.

In fact, smokers usually enjoy smoking so much, they can name their "favorite" cigarettes during the day. Think about this for yourself. Which cigarettes are your favorites during the day? Is it that first cigarette of the morning you smoke with your cup of coffee and muffin? Perhaps it's that cigarette you smoke in the car on the way home from a long hard day at work. Or maybe it's that one you smoke on your front porch after dinner while watching the sunset.

Now, why is smoking so enjoyable? Outside of the pleasurable feelings that cigarette smoking evoke inside of you, which we'll go over soon, cigarettes are likely participants in many positive events in your life. You associate smoking with happy times. You're out with friends at a baseball game, eating hot dogs, drinking beers, and smoking cigarettes. You're dining out with friends, eating appetizers, enjoying conversation, and smoking cigarettes. You're relaxing at home, holding your spouse's hand, watching the kids play, and smoking cigarettes. You link smoking to enjoyable events in your life and, thereby, smoking itself becomes more enjoyable.

As an experiment, pay attention to your thoughts the next time you're out of your house on a night when one of your favorite television shows airs. Or purposely go out to dinner on the same night as a "big game" or sitcom cliffhanger. And don't set your VCR of TiVo-that's cheating. Just try to accept the fact that you're going to miss that show. No matter how much fun you may be having, I'll bet your thoughts are placing you back at home on your comfortable couch watching that television. I'll bet you miss entire blocks of conversation thinking about that show you're missing.

The same thoughts apply to your favorite cigarettes. I'm sure you've all experienced those jitters when you've eaten in a non-smoking restaurant and couldn't enjoy that post-dinner cigarette. I'm sure your thoughts have drifted during long morning meetings at work that interfere with your usual time for a smoke break; you picture yourself out back smoking away, conversing gleefully with your fellow smokers.

This is one of the reasons why people fail to quit smoking so often. Even though you know deep down that smoking is bad for your health, it's fun; why would you want to stop doing something that's so fun? Cigarettes are one of the few negative things in this world that people can call a favorite. Think back on your life and try to remember a favorite pain, or a favorite car accident, or a favorite hurricane. Hopefully, you can't. But you can name your favorite cigarettes. Paradoxical, but true.

Availability

The second reason people fail so often is cigarettes are so readily available. They're everywhere. Usually they're in your front pocket, or in your purse, or in your car, or on the kitchen table. If they're not, I'm sure you have a reliable network of friends and co-workers whom you can ask for one. If they're not around, you can get them from a deli, a gas station, convenience store, or drug store. In fact, in the drug store the cigarettes are usually right behind the cashiers, while the smoking cessation aids are way in the back of the store by the pharmacist. You can likely name a few places within walking distance from your place of work or residence that sell cigarettes, and a few more on the road you take to work every day. In our society, cigarettes are unavoidable.

And it's not just cigarettes themselves that are everywhere. Ads for cigarettes are everywhere, too. Drive down a highway and count the number of billboards with larger-than-life promotions for cigarettes. Leaf through a popular magazine and count the number of ads for cigarettes. These ads, too, are unavoidable. Thinking back, these ads may have encouraged you to start smoking in the first place.

It's relatively easy to stop doing something, or eating something for example, if it's unavailable to you. If you're trying to lose weight, you don't go to the bakery as often. But if you go to someone's house for dinner and they put a nice rich piece of cake right in front of you, you may be hard-pressed to refuse to eat it. Since cigarettes are unavoidable in our society, the temptation for a smoker to smoke is constant.

Peer Pressure

The third reason people fail so often has haunted us since our days in elementary school. It's the same force that drove us to make fun of the new kid in class and make him cry. The same force that made us skip homeroom to play video games at the corner drug store. The same force that urged us to drive our parents' cars to the mall without permission, and without a license. It's simple peer pressure.

Think about it. The day's done. It's Friday. Time to go out with friends. A bunch of you are trying out a new restaurant in town, and then going for drinks. You arrive at the restaurant, sit down with your friends, and enjoy a wonderful dinner. You order yourself a cup of coffee. You lean back in your chair, stuffed to the gills, and what do you see? All of your friends are lighting up cigarettes right in front of you. One of them extends his lighter to you, ready to light you up. And here you are trying to quit. Not gonna happen. You know deep down that you'd like nothing better than to enjoy a cigarette with that cup of coffee. Besides, everyone else is smoking at the table, and you don't want to be the odd-man-out, the party-pooper, the kill-joy. So you have this one cigarette-but only this one, right?

Follow me here. After dinner, you're all off to the bar for drinks. You get out of your car, walk into the bar, and you're hit with a wave of second-hand smoke as you open the door. You look around to see everyone smoking-not just your friends, but *everyone in the bar*. Now what? You can't just turn around and go home; you're out with friends, having a great time. You can tell them that you're trying to quit, but then they may single you out, or make fun of you, or try even harder to get you to take a cigarette. You finally decide to try quitting again tomorrow, and join in with a cigarette. It's homeroom all over again.

Cigarette smoking in some ways is a societal choice, fraught with sociologic implications. You smoke, and your friends smoke. You all smoke together; it unifies you to a degree, just like watching football games together, or playing cards together, or going shopping together. If, for example, you decide to stop watching football, you necessarily break from the group a bit; the rest of the group will be sharing in an experience from which you've removed yourself. Faced with this possibility, you're more likely to sit through the football game with your friends. You may not enjoy yourself, but you're still with the group. The same idea applies to cigarette smoking. By not smoking with your friends, or co-workers, or whatever the case may be, you necessarily separate yourself from the group by refusing to join in a shared experience. To avoid feeling isolated or uncomfortable, you continue to smoke.

We never quite outgrow peer pressure. It continues to apply its negative influence through to adulthood. It makes you buy a two-seater when you know you need a mini-van. It makes you eat potato chips and beer when you know you need more fiber. And it makes you fail to quit smoking.

Your Brain

The fourth reason people have difficulty quitting is so hard to believe, it's a wonder that anyone is able to quit at all. Your brain is telling you to keep smoking. We've always been taught to listen to our brains. Our brains tell us what to do at every moment of every day. Our brains help us figure out what's right and wrong. The unfortunate fact, however, is that your brain doesn't want you to stop smoking.

The reason your brain wants you to keep smoking is because your brain needs nicotine. This fact is the basis of the addiction to nicotine, one of the most addictive substances in the world. The first records of the existence of nicotine date back to 6000 B.C. While nicotine typically comprises five percent of a nicotine plant, it nearly completely contributes to the addictive potential of cigarettes.

When you smoke cigarettes, you take in a small dose of nicotine, which reaches your brain in about ten seconds. The effects of nicotine on your brain are several. First, nicotine travels to your brain and activates signaling pathways that wake you up and make you feel more alert. If your brain is constantly exposed to nicotine, it eventually makes more pathways for the nicotine to use. Other chemicals use these pathways, too, but their amounts in the brain aren't even close to the amount of nicotine in a smoker's brain; these small amounts wouldn't signal the need for more pathways. Imagine a small country road traversing a one-horse town that handles very little vehicular traffic. There's no need to change the road architecture because so few cars use the existing road. Now imagine a very large shopping mall is built in the town. All of a sudden, thousands of cars are congesting this one small road, traffic is backed up for miles and no one's getting to the mall. The logical solution would be to create more roads, so that more cars can get to the mall. The same thing happens in your brain when it's exposed to nicotine. Pathways that usually see an easily manageable amount of activity are suddenly pummeled with large amounts of nicotine; in response, the brain makes more pathways to handle the increased load. At the end of these pathways are centers of the brain that wake you up and keep you alert and focused. Now that lots more signals can reach these areas of the brain, you feel much more awake and alert. Also, if you smoke continuously over several months and years, your brain gets used to this increased amount of activity, which then becomes the norm as far as your brain is concerned.

The problem here arises when the number of signals decreases. After you smoke a cigarette, nicotine lingers in your brain for about two hours. For those two hours, those pathways are charged with activity, and you feel energized and focused. After that time has elapsed, these pathways see much less activity, so these centers of your brain become relatively inactive. You feel sluggish and distracted. Furthermore, your brain notices a decrease in the usual flurry of activity in these centers. Imagine a shop owner in our shopping mall. Suddenly, fewer people are coming to the mall. Something is needed to attract more customers. Some lure is required. "Let's have a sale," declares our creative shop owner. Traffic picks up, and the mall is busy once again.

Now, you ask, what lure does our brain use to attract more nicotine? Very simple, bribery. To understand this, we need to introduce the second and third effects that nicotine has on the brain. In the second step of nicotine's influence, the increased activity of brain pathways, in addition to making you feel more alert and focused, stimulates other centers in the brain that make you feel happy. Alcohol and illicit drugs work in the same way. Next, through the release of other chemicals, your brain sets up a memory of the feelings you experienced while the nicotine was in your brain. The "lure" your brain uses is the memory of the wonderful way you felt after you smoked your last cigarette. Imagine, here you are feeling distracted and lackluster after not having a cigarette for a couple of hours. Your brain taunts you with memories of feeling energetic and happy, and reminds you that you can feel that way again if you smoke another cigarette. It's bribery, plain and simple. How can you expect to combat peer pressure and subversive advertising when your own brain is working against you?

Stress

A fifth reason for people to resume smoking, one of the strongest prods for a return to smoking, is stress. As I've stated many times, attempting to quit smoking is very difficult; quitting in itself is very stressful. Smoking cessation works best when it's your only life stressor. In general, stress can become insurmountable if it comes from several different sources at once, be them familial, social, or work-related. It's likely that of all the stressors that one can experience, quitting smoking is the easiest to resolve-just start smoking again. For example, say you take a trip to Las Vegas and lose all your money in the casinos. You don't even have enough money to buy a bus ticket home. Would it be easiest to go try to win some money back in the casinos with what little money you have left in your pocket, admit to your spouse that you lost the money and plead for forgiveness, or start smoking again? Even if you have a few dollars left in your pocket, you can likely afford a pack of cigarettes. At least by smoking again, you can remove one stressor from the pile.

Now, stress is unavoidable in most situations. Stressful situations can occur unpredictably in life, not allowing you the time to develop specific stress-reducing strategies. Plenty of smokers, at times, will smoke to relieve stress. And, sometimes, ex-smokers will return to smoking to relieve the pressure of other life stressors.

Summary

So you see, you're truly alone in your fight to quit smoking. Quitting smoking will force you to combat even your own thoughts. Friends, advertisers, and even your own brain want you to keep right on smoking forever. This is why people fail so often. These factors are what make quitting so challenging. You truly face a tremendous battle against these strong influences.

But by the same token, this is why failing to quit is not necessarily as bad as you may think. We're always taught that failure is unacceptable, and that we must constantly succeed in society. But how could you not fail, given the myriad forces driving you to keep smoking? Would you feel like a failure if Gary Kasparov beat you in chess? He's the best chess player in the world. Would you feel like a failure if Andre Agassi beat you in a game of tennis? He's one of the best tennis players in the world. The odds are definitely stacked against you, but you can win out in time with persistence and courage.

One thing not to do if you fail is become discouraged and pessimistic. Like I've stated before, this is a very difficult challenge. Just because you've failed doesn't mean you've failed forever. Pick yourself up, review your strategies, and re-dedicate yourself to the cause. It's just like learning to ride a bicycle, or play a harmonica, or knit a sweater. At first, you may scrape your knees, or honk an ugly tune, or make one sleeve longer than the other, but eventually, you'll succeed. Same idea with quitting smoking. If you fail once, you need to try again; it may just take a few attempts before you ultimately quit for good.

One thing you absolutely need to do if you fail is to review the reason for your failure. This is extremely important in preventing further failures. Review in your mind the days and weeks, or months and years as the case may be, during which you were free of cigarettes. Try to identify any specific events, or occurrences, or stimuli that may have triggered your return to smoking. You need to extract these stimuli so that you can develop strategies to combat them the next time you attempt to quit smoking. For example, did a stressful situation arise that you couldn't prepare yourself for, causing you to start smoking again for stress relief? Did a bunch of your friends take you out for your birthday to your favorite pub, causing you to start smoking again? Review your list of triggers, and see if you can implicate any of them in your return to smoking. If you can, you need to create new strategies for dealing with them before your next attempt. If you can't, you may need to lengthen your list of triggers.

Another thing you absolutely need to do is pick a new quit date, soon. Some smokers, distraught with having reverted to smoking, may never again try to stop. You need to go back to your calendar and pick a new quit date. Give yourself at least a few weeks to smoke before you try to quit again, though. While you need to keep your level of motivation to quit high, not leaving yourself enough time to prepare again may easily lead to another failure. Smoke your cigarettes, lead your life, and re-review your reasons for quitting. Remind yourself of the negative health and societal implications of smoking. Remember the conversations you had with people who have stopped smoking. Re-dedicate yourself to quitting, and try it again.

The third assignment after you fail is to prepare yourself for the next attempt. Remember, even though you've failed, you're still technically in a phase of cessation, that called relapse. Maintaining this frame of mind is exceedingly important for your potential future success. By considering yourself a failure, you imply that your attempt has ended, and that you've failed to achieve your goal. In this light, you may never again attempt to quit, which would be a tremendous disservice to yourself. On the other hand, by regarding yourself as a "relapser", you acknowledge that a failure does not represent the end of your journey towards smoking cessation, but merely represents one bump in the road. And the road you're on must end in quitting smoking. By defining your return to smoking behavior in this way, as a relapse rather than a failure, you will remain focused on the overall quitting process, instead of the individual quit attempt, and will be more likely to attempt quitting again in the near future.

I need to exemplify this for you. Say you're sitting at your kitchen table trying to complete a 1000-piece puzzle of the Grand Canyon. You've been working at the puzzle for the past two hours, and have about 200 pieces placed; however, you're getting frustrated, and you're finding it difficult to place anymore pieces. You need to stop for a while, so you rise from the table. Obviously, your goal, that of completing the puzzle, has not been achieved. Failure would be picking up the 200 pieces you've already placed, putting them back into the box, and putting the box back onto the shelf, never to open it again. Relapsing would be like leaving the pieces on the table and returning later in the day to complete the puzzle. Depending on the complexity of the puzzle, you may need to "relapse" several times before finally completing the puzzle. Now do you see the difference? When you fail, you never complete the puzzle. When you relapse, however, you eventually finish the puzzle after several tries. In this way, if you consider yourself a failure at quitting smoking, you may never again attempt to quit. If you view yourself as a relapser, though, you accept that you can return at a later date to try to complete the task at hand, that of smoking cessation.

So don't get discouraged if you fail once, or twice, or even three or four times. Quitting smoking is very hard. If you fail, and if you still truly want to stop, just try again and again and again. Sooner or later, you'll quit for good. Just don't give up on yourself.

Bibliography

Abbot, N. C.; Stead, L. F.; White, A. R.; Barnes, J. Hypnotherapy for smoking cessation (Cochrane Review). *The Cochrane Library, Issue 2, 2003.* Oxford: Update Software Ltd.
http://www.cochrane.org/cochrane/revabstr/ab001008.htm

Acupuncture: History and Theory.
http://www.suresoft.com/health/healthpt/acupct.html

American Lung Association Fact Sheet: Nicotine Replacement Therapy. American Lung Association. June 2002.
http://www.lungusa.org/tobacco/replacement_factsheet99.html

American Lung Association Fact Sheet: Second Hand Smoke. American Lung Association State of the Air 2002. June 2002.
http://www.lungusa.org/tobacco/secondhand_factsheet99.html

Apostolos, Apostolopoulos. *Acupuncture treatment for smoking cessation, in 190 cases.* http://users.med.auth.gr/~karanik/english/smoke.htm

Bandolier Library. Acupuncture to stop smoking.
http://www.jr2.ox.ac.uk/bandolier/band72/b72-5.html

Bryan, William J., Jr. A History of Hypnosis. January, 1963.
http://www.infinityinst.com/articles/nartic.html

Cigarette Smoke and Kids' Health. Physicians for a Smoke-Free Canada. December 13, 2001. http://www.smoke-free.ca/Second-Hand-Smoke/health_kids.htm

Cigarette Smoking. American Cancer Society. October 18, 2002.
http://www.cancer.org/docroot/PED/content/
PED_10_2X_Cigarette_Smoking_and_Cancer.asp

East West Clinic. Introduction to Acupuncture Theory.
http://www.eastwest-mn.com/introduction_acupuncture_theory.html

Environmental Tobacco Smoke. Environmental Health Center, A Division of the National Safety Council. September 15, 2000. http://www.nsc.org/ehc/indoor/ets.htm

Environmental Tobacco Smoke: A Hazard to Children (RE9716). American Academy of Pediatrics, Committee on Environmental Health. April 1997. http://www.aap.org/policy/re9716.html

Fact Sheet No. 9. *Nicotine and Addiction.* July 2001. http://www.ash.org.uk/html/factsheets/html/fact09.html

Farley, Kristy. Tools to Help You Succeed. Health Center, Quit Smoking. http://health.discovery.com/centers/quit_smoking/articles/aids.html

Feely, Richard, Ear Acupuncture, History. http://www.drfeely.com/acupuncture/ear_2_history.htm

Figure. The Fagerström Tolerance Test. Adapted from Fagerström KO, Heatherton TF, Kozlowski LT. Nicotine addiction and its assessment. *Ear Nose Throat J.* 1991; 69:763-765. http://users.aol.com/fedprac/nicofig1.htm

Fishman, Jon. The History of Acupuncture. http://acupuncture.com/Acup/history.htm

Gourlay, S. G.; Stead, L. F.; Benowitz, N. L. Abstract of review: Clonidine for smoking cessation. November 29, 1996. http://www.nihs.go.jp/dig/cochrane/jp_9802/revabstr/ab000058.htm

Grieve, M. *Lobelia.* A Modern Herbal. http://www.botanical.com/botanical/mgmh/l/lobeli38.html

Hajek, P.; Stead, L. F. Aversive smoking for smoking cessation (Cochrane Review). *The Cochrane Library, Issue 2, 2003.* Oxford: Update Software Ltd. http://www.cochrane.org/cochrane/revabstr/ab000546.htm

Hypnosis History. http://www.hypnosis-tapes.org/hypnosis-history.htm

Kern, Mark F. *Stages of Change Model.* Addiction Alternatives. 2003. http://www.aa2.org/philosophy/stagemodel.htm

Lancaster, T.; Stead, L. F. <u>Silver acetate for smoking cessation (Cochrane Review)</u>. *The Cochrane Library, Issue 2, 2003*. Oxford: Update Software Ltd. http://www.update-software.com/abstracts/ab000191.htm

Lancaster, T.; Stead; L. F. <u>Mecamylamine (a nicotine antagonist) for smoking cessation (Cochrane Review)</u>. *The Cochrane Library, Issue 2, 2003*. Oxford: Update Software Ltd. http://www.update-software.com/abstracts/ab001009.htm

Lewith, George T. *Smoking.* Excerpted from <u>Acupuncture—Its Place in Western Medical Seience</u>. http://www.healthy.net/asp/templates/article.asp?ID=2034

<u>Lobelia (Lobelia erinus)</u>.
http://www.gardenguides.com/flowers/annuals/lobelia.htm

<u>Lobelia</u>.
http://www.healthandage.com/html/res/com/ConsHerbs/Lobeliach.html

Mark, Ruth. <u>Hypnosis, History</u>.
http://www.shs.springfield.k12.il.us/proj/hypnosis/history.html

<u>Mecamylamine hydrochloride</u>. Delmar, a division of Thomas Learning. 2001.
http://www.nursespdr.com/members/database/archives/
mecamylaminehydrochloride.html

<u>Mecamylamine: antihypertensive helps quit smoking</u>. Quitting Tobacco Information. 2002.
http://www.besmokefree.net/Quitsmokingprograms/Mecamylamine.htm

Meeker-O'Connell, Ann. <u>How Nicotine Works</u>.
http://www.howstuffworks.com/nicotine.htm

<u>Michael R. Weir</u> Hypnotherapy. *Brief History Of Hypnosis in Medicine*. September 21, 2002. http://www.mrwhypnotherapy.com/hypnosis_history.htm

Miller, Karl E. <u>Nortriptyline Used as a Smoking Cessation Adjuvant</u>. As quoted from Da Costa CL, et al. *Stopping smoking. A prospective, randomized, double-blind study comparing nortriptyline to placebo.* <u>Chest</u> *August 2002; 122:403-8.* http://www.aafp.org/afp/20030101/tips/13.html

Moses, Scott. *Fagerstrom Test for Nicotine Dependence.* <u>Family Practice Notebook</u>. May 26, 2003. http://www.fpnotebook.com/PSY81.htm

Nicotine Addiction. American Heart Association. 2002.
http://www.americanheart.org/presenter.jhtml?identifier=4753

Nicotine Substitutes/Nicotine Replacement Therapy. AHA Recommendation
and Advocacy Position, American Heart Association. 2002.
http://www.americanheart.org/presenter.jhtml?identifier=4615

Nicotine Substitutes: What To Expect. Yahoo Health, from the American Cancer Society. October 18, 2002.
http://health.yahoo.com/health/centers/smoke_free/2.html

Nicotine Withdrawal Symptoms & Recovery.
http://www.quitsmokingsupport.com/withdrawal1.htm

Non-nicotine based chemical treatments for stopping smoking.
http://www.bupa.co.uk/health_information/html/healthy_living/lifestyle/
smoking/non_nicotine.html

Not Many Smokers Kicking The Habit. ABC News Internet Ventures. 2000.
http://abcnews.go.com/sections/living/DailyNews/smoking1224.html

Olmstead, Richard, Ph.D.; John Kelly, B.A.; Christina Chhin; Paula Iwamoto-
Schaap; M.A., Damian Madsen, B.A.; Lorena Huerta, B.A.; Catherine Sarkisian,
M.D.; and Neil Hartman, M.D., Ph.D. Combined bupropion and mecamylamine
treatment for smoking cessation: A pilot trial. Veterans Affairs-Greater Los Angeles
Healthcare System. http://www.srnt.org/events/abstracts99/
Combined%20Bupropion%20And%20Meca.htm

OMA Position Paper on Second Hand Smoke. OMA Committee on Public
Health. http://www.oma.org/phealth/2ndsmoke.htm

Perennial Flower Information. Lobelia. http://www.backyardgardener.com/pren/
pg77.html

Polito, John R. Is acupuncture effective in helping smokers quit? April 11, 2002.
http://whyquit.com/whyquit/A_Acup.html

Prochazka, A.V.; Weaver, M. J.; Keller, R. T.; Fryer, G. E.; Licari, P. A.; Lofaso,
D. A randomized trial of nortriptyline for smoking cessation. Archives of Internal
Medicine, 1998 Oct 12; 158(18):2035-9. http://www.ncbi.nlm.nih.gov/entrez/
query.fcgi?cmd=Retrieve&db=PubMed&list_uids=9778204&dopt=Abstract

Questions About Chinese History. http://www.paradigm-pubs.com/
MediaCenter/Background/HisQues1.html

Research Report Series—Nicotine Addiction, What Is Nicotine? U.S. Department of Health and Human Services. November 25, 2002.
http://www.nida.nih.gov/ResearchReports/Nicotine/nicotine2.html

Rowley, Christine H. Cigarette Ingredients, "The List": Mindboggling. Smoking Cessation. http://quitsmoking.about.com/library/weekly/aa042301a.htm

Sayer, Richard. History of Hypnosis. http://www.clinicalhypnosis.sayer.org.uk/history.html

Second Hand Smoke and Your Family. American Lung Association, State of the Air 2002. June 2002. http://www.lungusa.org/tobacco/smosecondha.html

Secondhand Smoke in Your Home. National Center For Chronic Disease Prevention and Health Promotion, Tobacco Information and Prevention Source. April 14, 2003. http://www.cdc.gov/tobacco/research_data/environmental/etsfact3.htm

Sharma, Sat. Nicotine Addiction. January 21, 2003. http://www.emedicine.com/med/topic1642.htm

Shaw, M.; Mitchell, R.; Dorling, D. *Time for a smoke? One cigarette reduces your life by 11 minutes.* British Medical Journal, 320:53. January 1, 2000. http://bmj.com/cgi/content/full/320/7226/53

Silagy, C.; Lancaster, T.; Stead, L.; Mant, D.; Fowler, G. Nicotine replacement therapy for smoking cessation (Cochrane Review). Issue 2, 2003. http://www.cochrane.org/cochrane/revabstr/ab000146.htm

Silagy, C.; Lancaster, T.; Stead, L.; Mant, D.; Fowler, G. Nicotine replacement therapy for smoking cessation (Cochrane Review). *The Cochrane Library, Issue 2, 2003.* Oxford: Update Software Ltd.
http://www.cochrane.org/cochrane/revabstr/ab000146.htm

Smoking Among U.S. Adults. CDC. December 24, 1997.
http://www.cdc.gov/od/oc/media/fact/smok1995.htm

Stages of Change. University of Massachusetts, Preventive and Behavioral Medicine. http://www.umassmed.edu/behavmed/smok_cess/stage.cfm

Stead, L. F.; Hughes, J. R. Lobeline for smoking cessation (Cochrane Review). *The Cochrane Library, Issue 2, 2003*. Oxford: Update Software Ltd. http://www.cochrane.org/cochrane/revabstr/ab000124.htm

The Hypnotic World of Paul McKenna (excerpt). History of Hypnotherapy. Published by Faber & Faber. http://www.hypnohealing.fsnet.co.uk/page2.html

The Path To Smoking Addiction Starts At Very Young Ages. National Center for Tobacco-Free Kids. October 16, 2002. http://tobaccofreekids.org/research/factsheets/pdf/0127.pdf

The Science of Second-Hand Smoke (SHS). American Non-Smokers Rights Foundation, Americans for Non-Smokers' Rights. January 8, 2003. http://www.no-smoke.org/ets.html

The Transtheoretical Model of Behavioral Change. http://www.cba.uri.edu/Scholl/WebTexts/Notes/TTM.html

Thomas, Jim (pages maintained by). Acupuncture, Electro-acupuncture and HealthTouch. http://www.srv.net/~jxt/technical.html

Ussher, M. H.; West, R.; Taylor, A. H.; McEwen, A. Exercise interventions for smoking cessation (Cochrane Review). *The Cochrane Library, Issue 2, 2003*. Oxford: Update Software Ltd. http://www.cochrane.org/cochrane/revabstr/ab002295.htm

What You Can Do About Secondhand Smoke as Parents, Decision-Makers, and Building Occupants. U. S. Environmental Protection Agency, Indoor Environments Division, Office of Radiation and Indoor Air, Office of Air and Radiation, EPA Document Number 402-F-93-004, July 1993. May 15, 2003. http://www.epa.gov/smokefree/pubs/etsbro.html

White, A. R.; Rampes, H.;Ernst, E. Acupuncture for smoking cessation (Cochrane Review). *The Cochrane Library, Issue 2, 2003*. Oxford: Update Software Ltd. http://www.cochrane.org/cochrane/revabstr/ab000009.htm

White, Adrian R.; Resch, Karl-Ludwig; Ernst, Edzard. *A meta-analysis of acupuncture techniques for smoking cessation.* Tobacco Control. 1999; 8:393-397 (Winter). http://tc.bmjjournals.com/cgi/content/full/8/4/393

0-595-29046-9

Printed in the United States
22478LVS00006B/247